NOTHING REMAINS THE SAME

NOTHING REMAINS THE SAME

Rereading and Remembering

WENDY LESSER

Houghton Mifflin Company

BOSTON   NEW YORK

2002

For information about permission to reproduce
selections from this book, write to Permissions,
Houghton Mifflin Company, 215 Park Avenue South,
New York, New York 10003.

Visit our Web site: www.houghtonmifflinbooks.com.

Library of Congress Cataloging-in-Publication Data
Lesser, Wendy.
Nothing remains the same : rereading and
remembering / Wendy Lesser.
p. cm.
Includes index.
ISBN 0-618-08293-X
1. Books and reading. 2. Lesser, Wendy
—Book and reading. 3. Literature—History
and criticism. I. Title.
Z1003 .L54 2002
028'.9—dc21   2001051622

Book design by Melissa Lotfy
Typefaces: Palatino, Sackers Gothic

Printed in the United States of America

QUM 10 9 8 7 6 5 4 3 2 1

For my parents and my son

The authors and the books that have, as we say, done something for us, become part of the answer to our curiosity when our curiosity had the freshness of youth, these particular agents exist for us, with the lapse of time, as the substance itself of knowledge: they have been intellectually so swallowed, digested and assimilated that we take their general use and suggestion for granted, cease to be aware of them because they have passed out of sight simply by having passed into our lives . . . Without having abandoned or denied our author we yet come expressly back to him, and if not quite in tatters and in penitence like the Prodigal Son, with something at all events of the tenderness with which we revert to the parental threshold and hearthstone, if not, more fortunately, to the parental presence. The beauty of this adventure, that of seeing the dust blown off a relation that had been put away as on a shelf, almost out of reach, at the back of one's mind, consists in finding the precious object not only fresh and intact, but with its firm lacquer still further figured, gilded and enriched. It is all overscored with traces and impressions—vivid, definite, almost as valuable as itself—of the recognitions and agitations it originally produced in us. Our old—that is our young—feelings are very nearly what page after page most gives us.

— Henry James,
"Honoré de Balzac," 1902

People pretend that the Bible means the same to them at 50 that it did at all former milestones in their journey. I wonder how they can lie so. It comes of practice, no doubt. They would not say that of Dickens's or Scott's books. *Nothing* remains the same. When a man goes back to look at the house of his childhood, it has always *shrunk:* there is no instance of such a house being as big as the picture in memory and imagination calls for. Shrunk how? Why, to its correct dimensions: the house hasn't altered, this is the first time it has been in focus.

Well, that's loss. To have house and Bible shrink so under the disillusioning corrected angle is loss—for a moment. But there are compensations. You tilt the tube skyward and bring planets and comets and corona flames a hundred and fifty thousand miles high into the field. Which I see you have done, and found Tolstoi. I haven't got him in focus yet but I've got Browning. . . .

—MARK TWAIN,
in a letter to William Dean Howells,
August 22, 1887

ACKNOWLEDGMENTS

I cannot possibly acknowledge all the people who contributed something to the way this book turned out, since that would involve thanking just about everyone who has spoken to me about well-loved books over the last thirty or forty years. So I will confine myself to a few recent helpers. I am grateful to Rachel Cohen, for finding the Mark Twain letter that offered me my title; Irina Paperno and Yuri Slezkine, for their crucial linguistic assistance on the Dostoyevsky chapter; David Leventhal, for a timely and important conversation about *Vertigo*, and Tom Luddy and Robert A. Harris, for tracking down facts about the movie's history; Katharine Ogden Michaels, whose advice on the "Young Woman's Mistakes" chapter was both sympathetic and corrective; Gary Wolf, whose comments and questions helped me wrestle with the Henry Adams material; Simone Di Piero, who sent me back to Shakespeare; Thom Gunn, with whom I shared many lunch conversations about our favorite rereadings; Ren Weschler, who arranged several opportunities for me to try out early drafts on attentive audiences; and Stephen Greenblatt, Tom Laqueur, and Robert Pinsky, who recommended my project to people who could support it. The Open Society Institute and Columbia's National Arts Journalism Program gave me generous fellowships during the writing of this book. My agent, Gloria Loomis, my editor, Pat Strachan, and my manuscript editors, Camille Smith and Liz Duvall, lent their calming intelligence to the publication process. Arthur

Lubow, always my first reader, read each chapter as I wrote it, and Tim Clark responded intensively to a draft of the whole manuscript; between them, they have left their fingerprints on just about every page, though they bear no responsibility for the errors or eccentricities, which are completely my own. I also want to thank my sister, Janna Lesser, and my husband, Richard Rizzo, who were my companions in much of the reading I describe here—she mainly during my early decades, he mainly during the more recent ones, though their jurisdictions have certainly overlapped. My mother, Millicent Dillon, and my father, Murray Lesser, are those from whom I received the gift of reading for pleasure, and my son, Nick Rizzo, is the one to whom I in turn transmitted it. This book is dedicated to them.

CONTENTS

NOTHING REMAINS THE SAME

REFLECTIONS

I**T BEGAN**, as things often do for me, with Henry James. I had nothing new in the house to read (a recent spate of bad fiction having destroyed my appetite for buying new books), so I searched my shelves and idly chose *The Portrait of a Lady*, a book I hadn't picked up in twenty years. Rereading it turned out to be an astonishing experience.

I had first read this novel as an undergraduate, and had gone through it again as a graduate student of English literature. Both times I was too close in age to Isabel Archer to appreciate her properly, and both times I read largely for the plot. The fact that I already *knew* the plot the second time around did not deter me: at the age of twenty-six, I still zoomed, suspense-driven, toward the final pages, as if only the ending counted.

But in your forties the journey begins to matter more than the arrival, and it is only in this frame of mind that you can do justice to Henry James. (I say this now, but just watch me:

I'll be contradicting myself from the old-age home, deploring my puerile middle-aged delusions about James.) At forty-six, no longer in competition with Isabel, I could find her as charming as her author evidently did. Moreover, having *had* a life, with its own self-defined shape and structure, I was more sympathetic with Isabel's wish to acquire one. As a young person, I only wanted her to marry the lord and get it over with. Now I understood that nothing ends with such choices—there are always additional choices to be made, if one's life is to remain interesting.

I cared less, this time through, about what decisions Isabel made than about how and why she made them. And this, in turn, gave me far more patience with the length and complexity of James's sentences. Once, perhaps, I had viewed them as pointlessly extended or merely ornate; now they were useful keys to the pace and method of Isabel's subtly complicated mind—so that whereas I used to be tempted to skip ahead, I now wanted to saunter through the commas, linger at the semicolons, and take small contemplative breaks at the periods. The book was much better than I had remembered it. More to the point, I was a much better reader of it. Both pleasure and understanding came more easily to me.

The idea that a simple rereading could also be a *new* reading struck me with the force of a revelation. It meant that something old wasn't necessarily outdated, used up, or overly familiar. It offered an escape route, however temporary, from problems that were both personal and cultural— my own creeping middle age, the prevailing fin-de-siècle tone of fashionable irony, and above all the speeded-up, mechanized, money-obsessed existence that had somehow become our collective daily life. Like many others before me (including, I noted wryly, Henry James), I felt menaced by too-sudden change, as if something I held dear were about to be taken away from me, or perhaps had already been taken away when I wasn't paying attention. I felt . . . But I needn't elaborate. You were there. You lived through it too.

My own situation differed somewhat from the average, in that I had purposely constructed for myself a life that was marginal to and therefore shielded from the clamoring demands of the marketplace. Well, "purposely" may not be the right word; in fact, one function of this book will be to examine in some detail how little "purpose" one can have, at fifteen or twenty or twenty-five, in imagining or projecting a life. But let us say that, for whatever reason, I found myself in the luxurious position of being able to reread. I had the necessary background—that is, I had read a lot of books when I was younger—and what's more, I had the necessary time.

Time is a gift, but it can be a suspect one, especially in a culture that values frenzy. When I began this book, almost everyone I knew seemed to be busier than I was. I supported myself, contributed my share to the upkeep of the household, and engaged in all the usual wifely and motherly duties and pleasures. But still I had time left to read. This was partly because I incorporated reading into my work life (I run a quarterly literary magazine), and partly because I worked very efficiently (I run my *own* quarterly literary magazine, so there's no busywork whatsoever: no meetings, no memos, no last-minute commands from the higher-ups). I had constructed a life in which I could be energetic but also lazy; I could rush, but I would never be rushed. It was a perfect situation for someone who loved to read, but it was also an oddball role, outside the mainstream—even the mainstream of people who read and write for a living. How often have you heard an editor or an academic or a journalist say, "Oh, I wish I had the time to reread *Anna Karenina*!" (or *Middlemarch*, or *Huckleberry Finn*, or whatever beloved book rises to the surface of one's memory)? Well, I thought, *I* have the time. I could reread on behalf of all of us.

Of course, it never really turns out that way in practice. Nothing demonstrates how personal reading is more clearly than rereading does. The first time you read a book, you might imagine that what you are getting out of it is precisely what the author put into it. And you would be right, at least in part. There is some element of every aesthetic experience, every *human* experience, that is generalizable and communicable and belongs to all of us. If this were not true, art would be pointless. The common ground of our response is terrifically important. But there is also the individual response, and that too is important. I get annoyed at literary theorists who try to make us choose one over the other, as if *either* reading is an objective experience, providing everyone with access to the author's intentions, *or* it is a subjective experience, revealing to us only the thoughts in our own minds. Why? Why must it be one or the other, when every sensible piece of evidence indicates that it is both?

Rereading is certainly both, as I was to discover. You cannot reread a book from your youth without perceiving it as, among other things, a mirror. Wherever you look in that novel or poem or essay, you will find a little reflected face peering out at you—the face of your own youthful self, the original reader, the person you were when you first read the book. So the material that wells up out of this rereading feels very private, very specific to you. But as you engage in this rereading, you can sense that there are at least two readers, the older one and the younger one. You know there are two of you because you can feel them responding differently to the book. Differently, but not entirely differently: there is a core of experience shared by your two selves (perhaps there are even more than two, if you include all the people you were in the years between the two readings). And this awareness of the separate readers within you makes you appreciate the essential constancy of the literary work, even in the face of your own alterations over time—so that you begin to realize how all the different readings by different people might nonetheless have a great deal in common.

This thing that I am calling "rereading" only succeeds under certain circumstances, and part of my effort here has been to locate those cases where the circumstances prevail. The book must, in the first place, be a strong one—not just a memorable one (though that is crucial), but also strong enough to hold up under the close scrutiny of a second look. It would be tedious to have a series of chapters recording how disappointing it was to reread this or that favorite work of science fiction or adventure or humor or romance (not that these categories would inevitably prove disappointing —but they do seem to be the categories in which youthful enthusiasm most often led me astray). I also hoped that each chapter would say something different—about the process of rereading, or the nature of growing older, or the quality of a work of art, or my own personality, or (preferably) all of the above. As both reader and writer I felt anxious to avoid mere repetition, which is not at all the same as rereading.

And then, of course, I had to remember the first reading well enough to get something new out of the rereading. This, unfortunately, eliminated some otherwise ideal candidates. For instance, I recently reread *The Charterhouse of Parma*, this time in Richard Howard's excellent new translation. I could remember exactly the circumstances surrounding my first reading: it was the late fall of 1984; I was staying at the Villa Serbelloni in Bellagio, and Stendhal's book was there in the library (having been acquired because of its associations with the region, no doubt); I was working on my own first book; and I was pregnant with my first and only child. Rich material for recollection, you would think. The problem is, I couldn't recall the slightest thing about the book itself. It was as if, on my recent rereading, I were coming across the Stendhal novel for the very first time—a tribute to the translator, perhaps, and a great pleasure in any case, but no help at all to my rereading project.

Sometimes I selected a book on the basis of its obvious

appropriateness to my topic, only to discover that my re-reading failed to produce a useful chapter. *The Interpretation of Dreams*, for example. What could better represent our collective readerly unconscious than this work that had permeated my generation's sensibility long before we ever read it? At twenty, I had devoured Freud's book with fascinated hunger, as if I both knew and yet didn't know everything it had to tell me (a perfect example, I remember thinking, of "the uncanny"). On my first reading the book had caused me to dream intensely, and to write down my dreams; perhaps that would happen again. And how appropriate it would be, I felt, to reread it on the hundredth anniversary of its 1900 publication date. But all to no avail. My primary, insuperable experience when I attempted to reread *The Interpretation of Dreams* was one of annoyance. Why had Freud mucked up his lovely approach to dream interpretation with that rabid insistence on the theory of wish fulfillment? And why was he such a tyrant about it? Bristling under the yoke of his oppressive manner, I tried another translation, but with no better results. It would be unpleasant, I finally decided, for readers to hear me yammering on against Freud's authoritarianism—after all, this is hardly news—and it would be even more unpleasant for me to do the reading and writing involved in constructing such a chapter. Since I rely on pleasure to fuel my criticism (though sometimes it's thwarted pleasure, in the case of negative criticism), I had no choice but to drop the book.

Some books, precisely because they seemed so appropriate, were never under consideration to begin with. *David Copperfield* and *Remembrance of Things Past* are both quite explicitly novels about rereading—so much so that I felt it would be redundant to examine them in this light. Besides, I had written about Dickens in every previous book of mine, and it seemed only reasonable to give him a rest.

The rules I cobbled together, in the end, were hardly onerous, but they were strictly enforced. I had to have done my first reading when I was "young"; in other words, I needed to be coming at the work anew as an altered, older self. I had to remember the first reading well enough to draw the comparison—viscerally remember it, not just remember that I had done it. And I had to get something new out of each individual rereading, some fresh idea or experience that had not appeared before, in order to make the chapters sequentially interesting. If I could do all this, I felt, I would have a book about rereading. It would be necessarily personal, with criticism merging into autobiography, but I hoped that it would not be *merely* personal—that what I had to say would find an echo, or at the very least a nod of assent, in the minds of other readers.

It has occurred to me that the danger of such a project is the danger of all escapism: we flee into the past because we can no longer tolerate the present. But one cannot actually live in the past, and I am certainly not ready to stop living. I never intended my rereading book to be a purely conservative measure, keeping out the new in favor of the old; I didn't ever stop reading new books while I was working on this project. For both professional and personal reasons, I can't imagine choosing not to read any new books. (By "new" I mean new to me: not necessarily books that have just been published, but books which I have only now encountered for the first time, whether they are just out or hundreds of years old.) And in fact my rereading project, far from making me shun new books, stimulated my desire for all kinds of reading. During the same time I was reading *Don Quixote*, for instance, I was also reading *The Letters of Henry James*, in Philip Horne's new edition; Shirley Hazzard's memoir *Greene on Capri*; J. M. Coetzee's *Age of Iron*, which I turned to after finishing his more recent *Disgrace*; Philip Roth's *The Human Stain*; and Alberto Moravia's *Contempt*. Of these, only *Age of Iron* turned out to have a direct bearing on my *Don Quixote* chapter, and that was purely by chance, but the stew into which they all went was, nonetheless, necessary to my writing. I suppose what I mean is that I needed to feel a life of letters going on around me—drawing from past works all the time, but also creating new ones every year, every minute—in order to feel that a book about reading was worth writing.

I did not set out to draw any general conclusions about rereading. General conclusions, I often feel, are the enemy of perception, at least in the literary field. To the extent that you can actually sense what is going on in a work of literature, you are sensing something more particular even than life itself (since life tends to have more repetition, more boredom, more plain old dead space than good literature usually does). But I did, in the course of producing this book, come upon one idea or image or tendency—I don't know exactly what to call it—that repeated itself over and over again. That was the idea of vertigo. There is something inherently dizzying in the effort to look at a still work of literature from a moving position—that is, from two different points in time. And this vertiginousness seems to be linked, in turn, to our directional sense of time's passage, to the poignancy of the fact that time only goes one way. There is some parallel, I can't help feeling, between that kind of one-wayness and the one-wayness of the relationship between a reader and a book. The characters in a novel can speak to us, but we can't speak to them—just as our younger selves can be heard and understood by our older selves, but not vice versa. These are not, of course, identical situations, but they are close enough to make us temporarily lose our balance. Or so I found when I looked at what Borges had to say about Cervantes, Hitchcock about the past, Wordsworth about childhood, McEwan about time . . . and so on down the list of artists I examine here. They all talked about vertigo, which is also, probably, the best word to describe what I felt when I looked again at the books I had first read a long time ago.

THE FIRST NOVEL

I AM CERTAINLY NOT the only person to have reread *Don Quixote*. It was done, most famously, by the fictional Pierre Menard, the Borges character who immersed himself so deeply, so thoroughly, and so intensively in Cervantes' masterpiece that he was able, at long last, to write a few chapters of it on his own—not from memory, but by having become its author anew. It was also done by the very real William Dean Howells, who wrote in a 1919 issue of *Harper's Magazine*, five months before his death, that "within my eighty-second year I have read *Don Quixote* with as much zest as in my twelfth year." Twelve seems young for a first reading, but Pierre Menard, too, started early: "When I was ten or twelve years old, I read it . . ." So it should not be surprising that I, when I first read *Don Quixote*, was eleven.

Still, it does surprise me. What did I imagine I was doing? Howells's "zest" would indicate that this primordial novel was once viewed as a childishly thrilling adventure book, like *Kidnapped*, say, or *Kim*. Is that what I thought I was getting? More likely I amalgamated it with T. H. White's *The Once and Future King,* that modern retelling of the King Arthur tales, which I read at about the same age. Knights of the Round Table, Knight of the Mournful Countenance—who knew the difference? How was I to know that the Cervantes book was an anti-chivalric epic, a parody of traditional knighthood adventures, when it sounded to my ears so much like them?

But that simplifies both my own response and Cervantes' intentions. He meant the novel to be taken on at least two levels—as the straightforwardly amusing antics of a hopelessly incompetent knight, and as a wittily self-referential critique of chivalric literature—and I took it on both those levels. What's more, Cervantes' critique was a defense as well: he meant us to laugh at Don Quixote's folly, but also to despise those prim figures who wished to "cure" the Don by burning his books. I understood that. I also understood that Sancho Panza was both sensible and silly, that Don Quixote's sanity was as sad as his madness, and that the relationship between me and these two figures was far more complicated than the usual one that unites readers and fictional characters. When you are just starting out, it is easy to break or ignore the rules, because you often don't know what they are. Cervantes, inventing the novel from scratch, accomplished all sorts of things that later writers were too cautiously professional to try; and I, reading one of my earliest grownup books, was too young and inexperienced to be worried by the violations of form. In that sense, we were ideally matched.

It's hard to picture a seventh-grader lugging around the standard two-volume hardcover edition of Samuel Putnam's 1949 translation, but I'm pretty sure that's the one I read. I must have lugged it one book at a time, as I did this time through, opening and closing and storing and unearthing each five-hundred-page volume until both jackets became ragged with wear. But I doubt that the copy I read then even *had* a dust jacket; in fact, I can almost picture the dark, dull color of the cloth cover and feel its closely woven texture in my hands. I don't know whether the book came from my mother's shelves at home or from the school library. I do know I read some of it during classroom hours, because I can still conjure up the sense of a windowless wall near my right shoulder, student desks stretching in rows before me and to my left, and the big volume propped open in front of me as I came to the end of the last chapter. Was it a free reading period, or was I hiding in the back of the classroom so I could surreptitiously finish the book? No matter; what I remember are the tears that stung my eyes when Sancho Panza stood by his master's bedside and pleaded with him not to die, but to go back out into the fields with him ("Who knows but behind some bush we may come upon the lady Dulcinea, as disenchanted as you could wish"). And I remember how the tears brimmed over when Don Quixote answered, "In last year's nests there are no birds this year. I was mad and now I am sane; I was Don Quixote de la Mancha, and now I am, as I have said, Alonso Quijano the Good." I knew, even at eleven, that something important was being lost here— no, was being bidden farewell to. I was parting from *Don Quixote,* the book, as Alonso Quijano was parting from Don Quixote, his other, crazier, but somehow more engaging and lovable self, and the separation was not an easy one—as I discovered again this time through, when the same tears (though how *can* they be the same?) stung my eyes at forty-eight.

Emotionally, then, the book was all there for me the first time, and it came back to me, emotionally, in the same register. But if I had, as a child, the capacity to respond to *Don Quixote*'s humor and pathos—let us not say fully, since no reading can ever be complete, but at any rate adequately—I lacked something that would have allowed me to take a more accurate measure of its author's achievement. I lacked, at that point, a literary education.

Even a child can see that *Don Quixote* is a book about reading. For one thing, reading—the wrong sort of reading, or too much reading, or possibly just reading in general—is seen as the cause of the knight's affliction. But one new lesson I now draw from Cervantes' novel is that you can never do too much reading if your aim is to appreciate Cervantes' novel. With this rereading, it became apparent to me that *Don Quixote* contains or alludes to many literary works it could not have known about—works that were written between 1615 and now. This did not occur to me when I was eleven for the simple reason that I had not then read any of these other books. Nor did I necessarily think of *Don Quixote* when I read them for the first time. But things which caught my fancy on their own—the asylum theatricals in Middleton and Rowley's *The Changeling* or Peter Weiss's *Marat/Sade*, the meandering journey and mutually reinforced superstitions of the two characters in *Huckleberry Finn*, the eccentric idealism of the central figure in *The Idiot*, the way the second half of *The Executioner's Song* comments on the characters' reactions to the first half—all seem prefigured, now that I have read it again, by Cervantes' great work. Sometimes the influence is a direct one (I know for sure that Dostoyevsky was thinking of Don Quixote when he created Prince Myshkin) and sometimes it is not (I know with equal certainty that Norman Mailer had not read *Don Quixote* when he wrote *The Executioner's Song*). But that distinction matters surprisingly little, since "influence" seems a puny force compared to the one exerted by *Don Quixote*. The novel displays such an astonishing ability to anticipate its own future that one is almost tempted to give Cervantes credit for *everything* written after him.

To read *Don Quixote* as an adult is to have the rereading experience in its most potent, seminal form. I imagine that this is true even if you did not read the book as a child, because, by the time you are a grownup, you will be familiar with all the main characters and many of their adventures. Don Quixote, Sancho Panza, Dulcinea del Toboso, Rocinante, Saragossa, the Cave of Montesinos, windmills, blanket-tossings, a flying wooden horse . . . are these specific memories from my first reading, or snippets of the general culture, handed down to all of us through visual art, drama, music, and other works of literature? Like any direct encounter with an originary myth, going back to the book itself induces chills of uncanniness. When the aspiring knight-errant announces that he will henceforth be Don Quixote, his beloved will be known as Dulcinea, and his horse will be called Rocinante—when he comes up with the names in front of your very eyes—you feel almost as if you are present at Adam's naming of the animals. It is hard to believe there was ever a world that did not contain these figures, and it is equally hard to believe they are the inventions of a single writer, a mere mortal. Miguel de Cervantes may have created Don Quixote and Sancho Panza, but they got away from him immediately. And everything about *Don Quixote*—from the way the story comes to us through layers of narrators to the way Volume Two is essentially a commentary on, a rereading of, Volume One—suggests that Cervantes *knew* his characters would escape him in this way.

It is this knowingness, combined with an unusually warm, informal kind of intimacy, that makes the book so remarkable. I have heard *Don Quixote* called both premodern and postmodern, but neither label feels right. Premodernism implies a distance from us, a lack of sophistication, a quaint kind of ignorance, whereas Cervantes is *right there*, whispering in our ear, seemingly cognizant of everything that has happened to his book from the time it left his hands four hundred years ago until it came to rest in ours. And postmodernism always entails a certain level of strain—an embarrassed self-consciousness, an effort to blatantly entertain or just as blatantly alienate, a nostalgic longing for the real even as the patently fake is seen as the only acceptable result of an artistic undertaking. Nothing could be further from the delicate tone of *Don Quixote.*

I cannot begin to do justice to the complicated strategies whereby Cervantes surveys the relationship between the real and the imaginary, truth and pretense, history and fiction, or whatever you want to call these "opposing" categories which he wisely refuses to set in opposition to each other. His novel does not suggest that there is no real difference, finally, between truth and fiction; that would be the pusillanimous way out, and Cervantes has no desire to take it. On the contrary, the whole point of the deluded knight's crazy adventures hinges on the difference. But making the distinctions is never simple. Who does more harm to Sancho Panza: the fake knight who promises him a real island to govern if he comes along as knight's squire, or the real duke and duchess who temporarily give him a fake island to govern, mainly for their own amusement? Is it crazier to sing the virtues of a lady love one can never obtain, as the troubadour poets traditionally do, or to sigh for a beloved made up wholesale, as Don Quixote does with Dulcinea? Which is the greater lie: to dress up as a knight because one deludedly believes in the reality of chivalry, or to dress up as a knight because, as a neighborly gesture, one wants to fool Don Quixote into quietly returning to his home? Is a dream a lie? (This is the thrust of the Cave of Montesinos incident, to which both Sancho and the Don frequently recur.) Does a false statement given in response to other people's manipulations or deceptions carry the same moral weight as an outright lie? (Sancho Panza often finds himself in this situation.) What is the difference between a lie and a work of fiction? Do fictional works have real effects in the world? If not, why should we care about them? And if so, how dangerous are they, and what are the costs of attempting to censor them?

One of the lovely things about the Putnam edition is that it includes all the front matter which, in the Spain of Philip III, had to be attached to any published book: the certificates of price and errata, the licenses and "approbations" of various clerical and secular censors, and finally the royal privilege to publish, issued by the king himself. In the case of *Don Quixote*, these sound so much like narrative artifacts—like the layers of storytelling at the front of a Conrad novel, for instance, or like Cervantes' own invention of the Moorish narrator Cid Hamete Benengeli—that they make "Miguel de Cervantes Saavedra" seem like one of his own fictional characters, even as they testify to the historical conditions under which he was allowed to make a living as a writer. And because all the testimonials are unremittingly high-minded, attributing only the purest and most conventional motives to Cervantes' work, we begin to wonder just who is fooling whom.

Take the "approbation" by Maestro Joseph de Valdivielso, which appears at the beginning of Volume Two and praises Cervantes for "mingling jest with earnest, the pleasing with the profitable, and the moral with the facetious, dissimulating under the bait of wit the hook of reprehension. All this in pursuance of his professed aim, which is that of driving out the books of chivalry, from whose contagious and baleful influence he has done much to cleanse these realms through the employment of his fine and cunning wit." Is he *serious?* The minute you ask yourself this, you begin to focus on words like "dissimulating" and "cunning." Nothing, of course, did less toward "driving out the books of chivalry" than the publication of Volume One of *Don Quixote;* if we are to believe Volume Two, the first book ignited a new rage for chivalric reading in fashionable and unfashionable circles alike. But then, the maestro seems to realize that this is only Cervantes' "professed" aim, not his real one. Or does he? The censor's position is as indeterminate as the author's own, or as that of the village curate from La Mancha, who says of certain poetic works that he finds while sorting through Don Quixote's library: "These do not deserve to be burned like the others, for they are not harmful like the books of chivalry; they are works of imagination, such as may be read without detriment."

Among the many reasons *Don Quixote* has not dated is the fact that we are still having this discussion. Having written a book about murders and executions, argued fiercely for years about the inviolability of the First Amendment, and raised a teenage son who is allowed to sample pretty much whatever he wants on the cultural front, I am more than ever aware of how common the curate's concerns are. The questions are all the same as they were in Cervantes' time: Does the representation of violence in art beget violence in real life? Even if that connection can be demonstrated, is censorship the right response? How is the censor to distinguish between "harmful" works and commendable "works of imagination" which are no less violent—like certain passages from the Bible, Greek drama, Shakespeare's plays, or, for that matter, *Don Quixote?*

"Well," Maestro de Valdivielso might say, "but the violence in *Don Quixote* is slapstick violence, comic violence." I'm not sure what he gains if I grant this. It's true that *Don Quixote* is often funny in exactly the way a Marx Brothers movie is funny. The battle between Don Quixote and the Knight of the Mirrors (who says he has read Volume One of *The Ingenious Gentleman, Don Quixote de la Mancha,* and therefore wishes to prove himself a superior knight by vanquishing that novel's hero) plays out very much like the mirror pantomime between Groucho and Harpo in *Duck Soup.* And many of the conversations between Sancho and the Don— particularly those about mispronounced words, the relation of language to meaning, and the proper use of proverbs and sayings—could have been scripted as dialogue for Chico and Groucho. But there is a darker strain in Cervantes' slapstick as well, more like the melancholy comedy of Buster Keaton or Charlie Chaplin. There are permanent losses entailed in the pursuit of chivalric ideals—not just the four or five teeth that Don Quixote loses ("and a tooth is more to be prized than a diamond") but also the injuries he inflicts on others. "I do not know what you mean by righting wrongs, seeing that you found me quite all right and left me very wrong indeed, with a broken leg which will not be right again as long as I live," says one of his victims. And there are deaths, as well, produced by a too vigorous pursuit of the knightly code—notably in the tale of the unfortunate Claudia, who stabs her faithless fiancé through the heart, only to learn too late that he was faithful after all.

As Volume Two draws toward its close, the tone of the work becomes noticeably darker. The story of Claudia is bracketed by two incidents that, while they occupy the background, nonetheless color the whole atmosphere. In the first, Sancho Panza is standing in the woods when he feels something brushing his shoulder; he turns to look, and finds that he is surrounded by hanged men—legally strung-up criminals—whose bodies have been left dangling from the trees. And then later, when the knight and his squire reach Barcelona, they are invited to witness the operation of a ship's galleys: like "magic," the ship moves as the result of the rowers' backs being flayed. "What have these poor wretches done that they should be whipped like that," wonders Sancho, "and how comes it that this one man who goes along whistling there dares to punish so many of them? I declare, this is Hell or at the very least purgatory." Both violent incidents, the hanging and the flaying, are completely unconnected to Don Quixote's delusions. They cannot be blamed on books of chivalry. On the contrary, they are routine, accepted aspects of daily life. Still, Cervantes is able to feel and convey their shockingness.

These are not just my modern prejudices being aired here. It would be presumptuous to assume that this was the case, to believe that our ethical sensibilities had somehow advanced since 1615—as if moral insight were like medical practice, superseding all the old techniques. Morally speaking, Don Quixote lived in the age of iron, and so do we; there never has been a golden age of good behavior and probably never will be, which is why we dream about it through books like *Don Quixote*. ("'Sancho, my friend,' he said, 'you may know that I was born, by Heaven's will, in this our age of iron, to revive what is known as the Golden Age.'") When modern artists re-create Cervantes' myth, it is often for the purpose of commenting on this recurrent fact of our fallen nature—as J. M. Coetzee does, for instance, in his novel *Age of Iron*, where the role of the deluded knight is taken by a dying South African white woman, her squire is a homeless black man, and her ancient car, "like Rocinante," can barely climb a hill. As this old woman rails and rages against the effects of apartheid, she becomes more and more cut off from everything that had previously been her life. Is she the one who is crazy, or does the fault lie with her world? The answer to such questions, in the most truthful works of fiction, is never as simple as R. D. Laing would have liked it to be.

That sort of thought would never have struck me in 1963, when I was eleven. It's not just that I hadn't read R. D. Laing then. (Hardly anybody had; his heyday was a few years later.) More to the point, I hadn't given much thought, one way or the other, to the idea of crazy people. I never saw any, and the ones I heard about were all locked away in huge state asylums or otherwise kept out of sight.

Now, of course, everything is different. I suppose the changes can be traced back to the 1960s and 1970s, when it was decided that warehousing was not helpful to the insane, and large numbers of mental patients were released from the asylums. This was initially a good thing, in that the patients were supposed to go instead to halfway houses or other smaller, more familial places. But at about the same time the plug was pulled on public money for mental health care, so all the halfway houses got shut down too, and there was nowhere for the released patients to go. They ended up on the streets, and now, a generation later, those who have survived are still there.

If I saw a raggedly dressed, dirty-faced, nonsense-jabbering lunatic even once during my entire Palo Alto childhood, I have managed to obliterate the memory. My son sees such people every week of his life. Granted, we live in the city nicknamed Berserkeley, on a street favored by the meandering homeless. Still, my son's experience is not a rare one for a modern urban child. He knows all the local knights-errant by sight, and he can set his watch by the one who passes our house every afternoon pulling his two garbage-filled shopping carts.

I am not suggesting that all these ragged fellows are Don Quixote in modern dress. But the analogy does give one pause. And, on the whole, I would say that my daily experiences with Berkeley crazy people give me some sense of what might be going through the minds of the characters who encounter Don Quixote. Their two most common responses—anger and fascination—are both familiar to me.

To the extent that we, as readers, find Don Quixote's madness amusing or even interesting, we are sharing the sensibility of the people in the novel who, like the otherwise kindly and civilized duke and duchess, entertain themselves at his expense. If the second volume of *Don Quixote* is more enjoyable and entertaining than the first, it is also chillier in this respect: we, personally, are being gotten at, and the satire is cutting closer to the bone. The people who encounter the crazy knight in Volume One are simply annoyed at his craziness and its effects on them (his failure to pay for his lodgings, his destruction of other people's property, the physical injuries he inflicts, and so on). In their annoyance they are often brutal. Hence the frequency of beatings in Volume One, to the point where the plot becomes repetitive and the outcome of every encounter is one more lost tooth or bruised limb or facial cut for either Don Quixote or Sancho Panza.

In Volume Two, the response is much more sophisticated. The people, especially the aristocratic people, who meet Don Quixote in the second book have all, like us, read the first. They have been vastly entertained by the reports of his eccentric behavior, and they are happy to invite him into their homes so they can see more of it. Volume Two is much more comfortable for the knight and his squire; they sleep in soft beds, eat well, and get treated as visiting dignitaries. There is far less brutality than in Volume One, but in its stead is a kind of smiling cruelty that bears some relation to sympathetic understanding. (I'm thinking here of the distinction Bernard Williams draws when he says that "cruelty needs to share the sensibility of the sympathetic, while brutality needs not to.") Much of Volume Two is like an amateur play, a party charade, a series of scenes set up by the participants in order to fool the only two actors who are not in on the joke. Only Don Quixote and Sancho Panza think it is all real: the punishments, the trials, the rewards, the flattery. We know ("we" including the other players in the novel as well as the readers of the novel) that it is all a setup.

Over and over Cervantes tells us how much "enjoyment" or "amusement" or "pleasure" these high-born hosts derive from the antics of the foolish knight—antics which they themselves set in motion with their clever schemes, their accurate predictions of his responses. Apparently the desire to be amused by crazy eccentrics is widespread, infecting not just the aforementioned ducal pair but also one Don Antonio and his wife, "a beautiful lady of high station and endowed with wit and gaiety" who "had invited some of her women friends to come and show honor to her house guest and enjoy his unheard-of variety of madness." And it is widespread not only in the novel but in the culture at large. This is the period, after all, during which performances by institutionalized lunatics or village simpletons were deemed acceptable entertainment for aristocratic gatherings, or so one is led to believe by plays like *The Changeling* and *A Midsummer Night's Dream.*

But the fact that the practice existed in life does not make its inclusion in art merely conventional or morally invisible. The use of the performing madmen in *The Changeling* is meant to make us queasy, and so is the friendly, jolly exploitation of the knight and his squire in Volume Two of *Don Quixote.* To make sure we get the point, Cervantes inserts a crucial comment by his Moorish narrator: "Here, Cid Hamete remarks, it is his personal opinion that the jesters were as crazy as their victims, and that the duke and duchess were not two fingers' breadth removed from being fools when they went to so much trouble to make sport of the foolish." So we have had our wrists slapped after all. But the process doesn't stop there; Cervantes never lets you rest on your moment of moral self-awareness. It's not enough to say "How cruel of them to laugh at the insane," or even "How cruel of *me* to laugh at the insane." For at the very point when he expresses, with obvious approval, Cid Hamete's position, Cervantes also wants to move you along to a questioning of that position. Yes, the duke and the duchess are fools . . . but is being foolish the worst thing in the world? Can we live and enjoy our lives *without* ever being foolish? And isn't a great deal lost to us (including the appreciation of novels like this one) if we try to stamp out such foolishness?

Twenty-five pages before Cid Hamete's aside, we get a different perspective in a remark made by Don Antonio, the knight's other benevolent exploiter. Don Quixote, who has been staying with Don Antonio, has just lost a battle to the "Knight of the White Moon"—actually his La Manchan neighbor, the bachelor Sansón Carrasco, disguised in full chivalric regalia. It is all part of a humanitarian ploy to get the deluded Don to return home, which is the penalty that the victorious knight has exacted from the vanquished one. But Don Antonio was not in on *this* charade, and he is dismayed when he learns about it: "'My dear sir,' exclaimed Don Antonio, 'may God forgive you for the wrong you have done the world by seeking to deprive it of its most charming madman! Do you not see that the benefit accomplished by restoring Don Quixote to his senses can never equal the pleasure which others derive from his vagaries?'" This is selfishness incarnate. It's also pretty much the way we feel about the matter, or at least the way *I* feel. Perhaps for different reasons, but with much the same warmth as Antonio's, I find myself always in opposition to the "cure" camp. Whenever the curate, the barber, the housekeeper, the niece, and Sansón Carrasco come onstage, I know we are destined to hear more trite homilies about the evils of chivalric books. Like Don Antonio, I tend to be in favor of leaving Don Quixote as he is, and I'm pretty sure Cervantes encourages me to feel that way. Or rather, he encourages me at the same time as he points out the moral risks I'm taking: nothing is ever absolutely settled in *Don Quixote,* one way or the other, and even the novel's own pleasure is not unmitigatedly approved of.

But pleasure there is, in enormous doses. One of the terrific things about this book is that you can still feel, down the distance of four centuries, Cervantes' delight in this new toy he's discovered, the novelistic form. It can create characters out of nothingness and bring them to life! It can skip around geographically in the twinkling of an eye, without any pause for scene changes! It can report on private matters that took place between its characters when no one else was present! The illiterate Sancho Panza, when he learns at the beginning of Volume Two about the existence of Volume One, instantly realizes how amazing this literary form is: "He told me the story of your Grace has already been put in a book called *The Ingenious Gentleman, Don Quixote de la Mancha.* And he says they mention me in it, under my own name, Sancho Panza, and the lady Dulcinea del Toboso as well, along with things that happened to us when we were alone together. I had to cross myself, for I could not help wondering how the one who wrote all those things down could have come to know about them." Don Quixote's reaction is somewhat different. Since he has believed all along that his knightly quest is being thwarted by evil enchanters, he has no trouble incorporating this new form of magic, novel writing, into his worldview: "'I can assure you, Sancho,' said Don Quixote, 'that the author of our history must be some wise enchanter; for nothing they choose to write about is hidden from those who practice the art.'"

For us, the enchantments of the novel have become so routine as to be practically unnoticeable. As the psychoanalyst Adam Phillips said when reviewing a recent novel, "It is, after all, an effect of style to make this living in someone else's mind seem so natural, given that it is something we never, in actuality, do." *Don Quixote*'s style is the opposite sort: the novel spends little if any time inside its characters' minds, and it frequently reminds us what a very *un*natural thing we are doing when we get to know fictional characters. Distinctions that seemed clear to Cervantes have become murkier for us, and, in part because he did a lot to muddy those waters himself, it's very difficult for us to recover his freshness of perspective. As Borges (speaking through Pierre Menard) observes, "To compose the *Quixote* at the beginning of the seventeenth century was a reasonable undertaking, necessary and perhaps even unavoidable; at the beginning of the twentieth, it is almost impossible. It is not in vain that three hundred years have gone by, filled with exceedingly complex events. Among them, to mention only one, is the *Quixote* itself."

At the age of eleven, I was oblivious to much of what was innovative and unusual about *Don Quixote*. For all I knew, that was how they wrote books in those days ("those days" encompassing, in my mind, both the medieval period of chivalric literature and Cervantes' much later time—they had been collapsed, for me, into an undifferentiated past). I had read few if any nineteenth-century novels, so I had no firm expectations about novelistic form or plot construction or character revelation. I knew *Don Quixote* was a long book, and it felt like one, but what I didn't realize is that it felt even longer because of its nearly plotless, one-thing-after-another structure. Cervantes may have discovered the novel, but he had yet to discover suspense (though we begin to see the first glimmerings of it, in the form of more sustained plot development, in Volume Two). His newly minted form, if it borrowed anything from theater, took more from the vaudeville-like routines of *commedia* than from the Golden Age drama of his Spanish near-contemporaries. The desire to be entertained from one moment to the next, rather than the desire to reach an endpoint, is the readerly appetite he feeds. Not that he always feeds it with equal success: *Don Quixote* has its *longueurs,* especially in the first volume. When I was young, I skipped most of the poems that are sprinkled throughout the text; this time, after a brief struggle with my responsible-critic conscience, I did the same. The first time I read the book, it took so long to get through the initial volume that I had forgotten most of the minor characters and incidents by the time I reached its end, and the same was true this time.

Yet even here Cervantes anticipates me. If I was occasionally bored, it was apparently as nothing next to the feelings of Cid Hamete Benengeli, who (Cervantes tells us) had "a kind of grudge . . . against himself for having undertaken a story so dry and limited in scope as this one of Don Quixote." In the first volume the narrator attempted to rectify this problem by introducing a few irrelevant but diverting travelers' tales, but later he decided this had been a mistake, since "many readers, carried away by the interest attaching to the knight's exploits, would be inclined to pass over these novelettes hastily or with boredom, thereby failing to note the fine craftsmanship they exhibited." The self-criticism veiled as self-praise is incomparable, but what makes it quintessential Cervantes is the way it takes into account *our* feelings as well as the puppet author's.

If Cervantes rarely peeks into his characters' skulls, he frequently peers into ours, and the effect, especially in the second volume, is thrillingly intimate. Before we can have a fully formulated thought about his book, he has it for us, but he does it in such a witty, engaging, flattering way that we almost feel we have anticipated *ourselves*. Above all, Cervantes makes us aware that we are reading a printed object, and then he makes that awareness part of the book's plot. This produces an eerie sensation, in that the smaller universe, that of the novel, seems to have swallowed whole the larger universe in which we dwell.

When Sancho Panza first learns from Sansón Carrasco, for instance, about the existence of the printed and disseminated Volume One, they have a detailed conversation about the logical errors embedded in the text. This is a bit as if Dickens, Jane Austen, and Arthur Conan Doyle were to come back to life and begin debating with John Sutherland about his numerous challenges to their authorial consistency. But even more surprising is the way the discussion concludes. Sansón, after hearing Sancho's lengthy but finally unsatisfying explanation for the disappearance and reappearance of his stolen donkey, refuses to be placated.

> "That is not where the error lies," replied Sansón, "but rather in the fact that before the ass turns up again the author has Sancho riding on it."
>
> "I don't know what answer to give you," said Sancho, "except that the one who wrote the story must have made a mistake, or else it must be due to carelessness on the part of the printer."

And thus do the errors, whether authorial or typographical, get made a part of the permanent record. *Don Quixote* is so capacious that it can swallow even its own mistakes.

The effect of such strategies is to bring us to "the point of vertigo," as Borges says in his intriguing little essay "Partial Magic in the *Quixote.*" That vertiginous feeling will come up again: it is, I am convinced, the representative sensation of rereading at its most powerful, the feeling we get when two worlds (the child's and the adult's, the fantastic and the mundane, the life lived through books and the rest of life) are superimposed on each other. But here I want to focus on what Borges makes of that discovery. I believe it is one of the few places where he goes wrong—he who otherwise understood *Don Quixote* so well that rereading "Pierre Menard, Author of the *Quixote*" has almost become a necessary adjunct to rereading Cervantes' novel (so that Menard has, in a way, been granted his wish).

At the end of "Partial Magic," Borges asks:

> Why does it disturb us that Don Quixote be a reader of the *Quixote* and Hamlet a spectator of *Hamlet?* I believe I have found the reason: these inversions suggest that if the characters of a fictional work can be readers or spectators, we, its readers and spectators, can be fictitious. In 1833, Carlyle observed that the history of the universe is an infinite sacred book that all men write and read and try to understand, and in which they are also written.

This is a grand theory, but it strikes me as false—logically false, in its if-then assumption, and also false to the feeling that *Don Quixote* produces. For me, the novel's effect is one of enlargement, not reduction. My own sense of vertigo stems from the fact that the characters have stepped outside their realm into mine, and not the other way around. Through some inscrutable mechanism, they have become more real without my having to become less so. In any case, it's hard for me to understand how I would go about considering myself fictitious—but then, I have neither the desire nor the ability to see myself as a character in the mind of God. I don't think Cervantes asks us to adopt the God-as-author model, or even the God-as-history-as-author model. What he does instead is to suggest that the reality we share with Don Quixote—this ongoing reality of ours, this limited life, which can nonetheless contain at least one novel so much larger than itself—is more than enough of a wonder.

I could not love *Don Quixote* more than I did at eleven, but I can admire it more now. As a child I took its virtues for granted. Now I am amazed by the extent to which it anticipates so much, not only about its own fate as a book, but about novels and novel writing in general. In a much more informed and visceral way than when I was eleven, I comprehend how much time separates me from Cervantes, and that makes me all the more impressed by how cunningly he has closed the gap. His voice speaks directly to us, whatever our moment in history: to William Dean Howells in 1849 and 1919, to Jorge Luis Borges (or Pierre Menard) from 1909 onward, to me in 1963 and again in 2000. For this reason, perhaps, the process of rereading *Don Quixote* feels less like a transformation than is the case with other books; the difference between the initial youthful reader and the eventual older one seems comparatively small. And that is a relief, in a way. It works to counter the sense of romantic retrospection, of elegiac time-travel, that otherwise colors a book about rereading. After all, how seriously can one take the passage of a mere thirty-seven years, when Cervantes leaps over four hundred as if they were nothing?

ADOLESCENCE

WHEN I WAS THIRTEEN, my
three favorite books were *The Catcher in the Rye*, *Lucky Jim*,
and a rather obscure novel called *I Capture the Castle*.

I do not plan to reread *The Catcher in the Rye*. I just can't
bear to. If you think it's so important, *you* reread it. (But having had that thought, I couldn't resist taking a peek at the
first page of my teenage son's copy. The book's first sentence
is: "If you really want to hear about it, the first thing you'll
probably want to know is where I was born, and what my
lousy childhood was like, and how my parents were occupied and all before they had me, and all that David Copperfield kind of crap, but I don't feel like going into it, if you
want to know the truth." It did not escape my notice that,
over a distance of thirty-five years, Salinger's tone, even bits
of his own language and style, had invaded my refusal to
reread his book. I was impressed and somewhat amazed,
but not eager to read any further. So I didn't.)

Catcher aside, I am left with two oddly paired books.
Lucky Jim is a classic midcentury comic novel—Kingsley

Amis's first and, according to many readers (including me, at times), his best. If you tell people you are reading it, they will invariably say, "Isn't it wonderful? It's the funniest book I've ever read!" and then they will proceed to recite their favorite humorous bit from memory. Hardly anyone has read Dodie Smith's *I Capture the Castle* (or at least *had* read it, before J. K. Rowling, the Harry Potter author, championed it and gave it a spurt of new life). It too is a midcentury novel —first published in 1948—and it too is set in England. But whereas *Lucky Jim* fully inhabits the dour, constrictive postwar period, *I Capture the Castle* looks backward at a very different England, pre-war and prior. And while Amis's novel can be, and has been, enjoyed by men and women, teenagers and adults, Dodie Smith's is very much a book for overimaginative girls.

I am not the only overimaginative girl who loved both these books at once. Recently I got a phone call from my sister, who is two years younger than I am. She was calling to tell me about a dream she had just had. "Kingsley Amis was in it," she said, "and when I saw him I said, 'Oh, I just loved *Lucky Jim*—it was one of my favorite books as a child. Now, *what* was that main character's name?'" My sister was particularly amused at the dream's comic way of forgetting and remembering at the same time, and she even seemed somewhat abashed at having made this ridiculous *faux pas* in front of the demonstrably fabricated (and in fact dead) Kingsley Amis. But the dream also made her think about the book again, and before I could intrude with my own associations, she added: "That was a good book. I feel like reading it again. That and *I Capture the Castle*."

Perhaps one of the things we both liked about Dodie Smith's novel was that it was the story of two sisters. This I remembered; what I had forgotten, until I began to read the book again, was that they were the daughters of a writer. So were my sister and I. Granted, *I Capture the Castle*'s parental writer was a man, the highly acclaimed author of the

Joycean philosophical-poetical-modernist text *Jacob Wres-tling,* whereas ours was a woman, our divorced mother, whose delicate fictions had only just begun to be published in literary magazines. But these differences aside, certain parallels remained: the familiar need to leave the writer undisturbed behind closed doors; the sudden arrival and de-parture of stepparents; the sense of being the eccentric fam-ily in an otherwise normal community; and, not least, the de-sire on the part of the writer's children to become writers themselves.

The two sisters in *I Capture the Castle* are called Rose and Cassandra Mortmain. (You can imagine how people named Wendy and Janna Lesser might have longed for names like those. Reading, especially youthful reading, is always a com-bination of envy and wish fulfillment.) The older sister is beautiful, with red-gold hair; the younger, brown-haired sis-ter is merely intelligent. I had red hair, and I too was an older sister, so you might have expected me to see myself, how-ever unrealistically, as Rose. But in fact Janna and I both dis-liked Rose and admired, or at least sided with, Cassandra, as Dodie Smith clearly intended us to do.

It helps that she is the book's narrator, the seventeen-year-old "I" who is capturing for our benefit the run-down old castle in which the impoverished Mortmains live. She is also an appealing figure in her own right: a combination of Elizabeth Bennet and Jane Eyre, with a large share of some-thing else added in. A bookish girl, Cassandra would not be averse to the nineteenth-century comparison, and she even invokes it herself at one point, when she and Rose are talk-ing in their room before bed. "How I wish I lived in a Jane Austen novel!" Rose has just said, deploring the absence of eligible men in her life.

> I said I'd rather be in a Charlotte Brontë.
> "Which would be nicest—Jane with a touch of Charlotte, or Charlotte with a touch of Jane?"

This is the kind of discussion I like very much but I wanted to get on with my journal, so I just said: "Fifty percent each way would be perfect," and started to write determinedly.

Part of the charm of *I Capture the Castle*—and this too I had completely forgotten until I started to reread—is that it takes the form of Cassandra's journal. Usually I don't like epistolary or otherwise *in medias res* works of fiction. The structure always seems strained and at the same time insufficiently inartistic. Rather than bringing us closer to the characters, the false immediacy of the narrative usually puts us at a greater distance by making us notice the format. But Dodie Smith's novel has never had that problem for me, as illustrated by the fact that I didn't even recall the format, only the characters and much of their story and, intermittently, some individual scenes and phrases. Beginning to reread *I Capture the Castle* was like opening the front door to a house that I had visited very happily as a child but hadn't seen in years. The characters I encountered in those rooms (including the recollected reader, my younger self) were familiar enough to engender fondness, but not so well remembered as to be dull or predictable.

I'm afraid I can't say the same of *Lucky Jim*. Perhaps the problem is that I read it too well the first time around. Or, more likely, read it too often: I'm sure I must have gone through it three or four times in the course of a couple of years. Whatever the reason, Amis's sentences—especially the funny ones—are branded into me, so that reading the book now was a bit like hearing a well-told joke once too often. If I laughed, it was out of polite acknowledgment, not in surprised delight.

I can still remember the enormous pleasure I took, at age thirteen, in Jim Dixon's attitude toward his scholarly article, which Amis wickedly titled *The economic influence of the developments in shipbuilding techniques, 1450 to 1485:* "Dixon had read, or begun to read, dozens like it, but his own seemed

worse than most in its air of being convinced of its own use-
fulness and significance. 'In considering this strangely neglected topic,' it began. This what neglected topic? This
strangely what topic? This strangely neglected what?" I can
recall reading these lines both silently to myself and aloud to
others, though the spoken rendition was often muffled by
uncontrollable laughter. I imagine that, even before my recent rereading, I could have recited those last four sentences
pretty much word for word. Writing them down here, I can
still appreciate that they are beautifully constructed comic
sentences, as memorable as poetry. But that, in a way, is the
problem: I remember them too well, just as I remember Margaret's ghastly outfit (her paisley dress and quasi-velvet
shoes), Bertrand's annoying verbal tic ("You sam"), and Dixon's colossal hangover, down to the very detail about his
mouth having been "used as a latrine by some small creature
in the night, and then as its mausoleum."

Sentence by sentence, as my quotations indicate, *Lucky
Jim* is a far more polished book than *I Capture the Castle*. In
terms of cleverness, fluency, and pure love of the English
language, the writing can't be beat. Why, then, has it gone
dead on me, when the other book still engrosses?

I certainly haven't outgrown the subject matter. As someone who went through a Ph.D. program in English and only
belatedly abandoned academia, I might be said to have
grown *into* the subject matter of *Lucky Jim*. When I first read
it, as a teenager, I knew few if any people who taught in uni-
versities, so the direct hits at scholarly pomposities would
have struck me as amusing and far-fetched constructions.
Only now can I comprehend how faithfully Amis must
have been transcribing a perceived reality. Nor was I
equipped, as a child, to see how acutely he was examining
the whole question of class in England. The book is riddled
with it, subtly and richly burdened with it; but having
grown up in supposedly classless Palo Alto, and having
never been to Britain except through books, I had no way of

understanding this particular source of Dixon's resentment.

What I did understand was the strength of that resentment. A kind of withheld fury, a generally silent but nearly overpowering rage, lies at the heart of *Lucky Jim.* This is why the weakest scenes are the love scenes, while the best parts of the book are those about the objects of Dixon's ire: the sneaking oboe-playing Johns, the daffily malicious Professor Welch, and, above all, Welch's obnoxious son, "the bearded pacifist painting Bertrand." Resentment is what makes Dixon's ultimate theft of Bertrand's girlfriend and Bertrand's job so satisfying. It is not that those things are so good in themselves (the woman is little more than a physically attractive cipher, and the "private secretary" sinecure is even more vaguely defined), but that they represent something taken away from Bertrand—something he wanted and felt entitled to and yet didn't finally get.

The division between those with a sense of entitlement and those without can substitute, in the adolescent world, for class structure. That's why, at thirteen, I didn't need the concept of class to understand *Lucky Jim.* In the world I inhabited at that time, there were certain people who felt they deserved all the pretty girlfriends (or handsome boyfriends) and prominent social positions and general good luck, and to a great extent they were the people who got all those things. At thirteen, that's just how things were. It all seemed fated. But in *Lucky Jim* (whose title adjective, I now perceive, is absolutely crucial), that luck gets magically reversed. The underdog, the loser, ends up with all the chips, and the seemingly "superior" people are defeated. It's an adolescent's dream.

An adolescent's nightmare, too, because the primary negative feeling in the book is embarrassment. (The primary positive feeling is righteous vindication—a corollary, and outgrowth, of the suppressed rage.) Embarrassment—along with its variants, humiliation and shame—is the key teenage emotion. We never outgrow it entirely, and some adults live under its sway more than others. But almost no adult allows his life to be governed by embarrassment in the way that almost every adolescent does.

Repeatedly, in *Lucky Jim,* the potential doom that faces Dixon is humiliation. He burns up his own bedclothes during a weekend at the Welches' house, and then spends the rest of the novel sheepishly avoiding Mrs. Welch's attempts to confront him about it. He is pulverized with embarrassment at Margaret's admittedly grotesque attempts to discuss their "relationship," as it would now be called. At the novel's climax, he delivers a university-sponsored speech about Merrie England in a drunken haze, managing to mimic and thereby alienate every powerful person present —everyone, that is, who controls his job at the university, which he therefore loses. And even Dixon's prospective unemployment is fearful mainly as another form of humiliation, not all that different from the impoverished academic employment that keeps him in dingy lodgings and insufficient cigarettes.

When I was younger, all these experiences of shame had tremendous power for me. They were linked with, and in fact gave rise to, the uncontrollable laughter I still associate with this book. Humiliation punctured by humor: that was the mechanism by which *Lucky Jim* gave me so much pleasure. But the puncture alone survives, so that the novel seems to me now like a deflated balloon, something that was once tense with its own pressure but now lies in a soft, wrinkled, inert heap. With the loss, or at any rate the serious decline, of my own inherent sense of embarrassment, Amis's power to move me has sadly diminished. I can still enjoy the artfulness and concision of the book, but the emotions it once aroused have abandoned me almost completely.

The opposite is true of *I Capture the Castle.* I loved the book at thirteen for reasons that couldn't possibly have been apparent to me then, and now, looking back, I see exactly what they were. This is not because I have outgrown the book or have become more thoughtful than it is or have come to understand life better than it does, but because I now understand life in very much the way this book does. Peering back down the years through the telescope of *I Capture the Castle*, I see not only the girl who first read the book but also the woman she developed into, as if the book itself were in some way responsible for that development.

I can see myself, for instance, in almost all of Cassandra's various beliefs and preferences. "My imagination longs to dash ahead and plan developments; but I have noticed that when things happen in one's imaginings, they never happen in one's life, so I am curbing myself." "I wish I could have had that food when I wasn't at a party, because you can't notice food fully when you are being polite." "I always enjoy the different feeling there is in a house when one is alone in it." "I believe it is customary to get one's washing over first in baths and bask afterwards; personally, I bask first." "I like seeing people when they can't see me. I have often looked at our family through lighted windows and they seem quite different, a bit the way rooms seen in looking-glasses do." "Of course, what my mind's eye was telling me was that the Vicar and Miss Marcy had managed to by-pass the suffering that comes to most people—he through his religion, she by her kindness to others. And it came to me that if one does that, one is liable to miss too much along with the suffering." To what can I attribute the fact that I share these convictions? Did I, at thirteen, absorb the book so fully that it shaped my habits and superstitions as I grew older? Or was I drawn to Cassandra's personality precisely because it mirrored my own gradually emerging character? Or are her beliefs so widely held that *any* girl would have grown into them, in time?

That last possibility seems unlikely, especially in regard to how we take our baths. But still, there is something about the openness of Cassandra's personality, its capaciousness—

she is first and foremost a reader, so she has that in common with whoever is reading *her*. And, like her reader, Cassandra is shaped by what she reads. "Now I come to think of it, I am judging from books mostly, for I don't know any girls except Rose and Topaz," she muses. I, at thirteen, knew many other girls, but I knew very few who were as much like me as Cassandra was. And now I come to think of it, those qualities of hers which I share (liking to look in from the outside, abstractly valuing suffering as experience, being superstitious about imagining things, and so forth) are all the characteristics of a reader. I was already a reader, of course, when I first read *I Capture the Castle*, but at that age I could have had no idea how centrally books would occupy my adult life.

This is only part of the story, though. If *I Capture the Castle* is about being a reader and becoming a writer, it is also about how an individual existence unfolds. Does a life develop like a novel, with a distinct trajectory and a satisfying finish, or is it more meandering and uncertain? Because she presents her story to us as a series of journal entries, Cassandra's narrative has it both ways. We are treated to a sequence of shapely incidents and temporary conclusions—there is suspense, and fulfillment of suspense—but the story remains, at its close, open-ended.

I remembered that *I Capture the Castle* was about two English sisters who fell in love with two American brothers. What I did not remember, until I reached the very end of my rereading, was that Cassandra's love remains unresolved. She might eventually marry Simon or she might not; the journal ends before we can be sure. Yet this is not a tease. Rather, it is a practical acknowledgment of a truth elucidated by Cassandra midway through the novel—that satisfaction brings a form of sadness. "What I'd really hate would be the settled feeling, with nothing but happiness to look forward to," she thinks, contemplating her sister's impending marriage. "I think what I really mean is that Rose won't be *want-*

ing things to happen. She will want things to stay just as they are." Cassandra herself goes back on this statement when she falls in love: at that point she can imagine nothing better than the satisfaction of her desires. But the journal format allows both positions to stand equally, so that neither longing nor satisfaction gets the final accolade. One's philosophy, it turns out, depends in part on one's feelings, which can be frighteningly temporary. That is what *I Capture the Castle*, with its sense of a continuous present, beautifully captures.

And yet the book explores the past and the future too— or, to be more accurate, the past as recalled from an imagined future and the future to which the present shall become an imagined past. If Cassandra captures, she also, like Proust, recaptures; "recapture" is in fact one of her favorite words, appearing repeatedly in her journal entries about the near or distant past. And when she thinks of the future, it too contains this element of recapturing. "We were driving through Godsend and the early sun was striking the moss-grown headstones in the churchyard," she says in one of her more evocative passages. "I tried to realize that I shall die myself one day; but I couldn't believe it—and then I had a flash that when it really happens I shall remember that moment and see again the high Suffolk sky over the old, old Godsend graves."

I had not been to England when I first read *I Capture the Castle*, and I was not to go there—first to visit and then, for a few years, to live—until I had stopped reading and consciously caring about this book. But now I see that Dodie Smith's novel was in part responsible for the way I felt about England when I did eventually get there. It is hard to separate this single influence from my general bookishness: Jane Austen and Charlotte Brontë, not to mention C. S. Lewis and E. Nesbit, must be responsible, too. But there are certain elements of Englishness that I specifically associate with this book. I think I first learned to count the shillings in a pound and the pence in a shilling by reading this novel, and I *know* I learned from it that a guinea was worth a shilling more than a pound. By now all this once practical knowledge has itself become purely literary, since Britain has gone decimal; even an English child, today, would know about shillings only from books. But when I first visited England in 1970 they were still the coin of the realm, and to me it was like having a novel come to life.

One of the reasons *I Capture the Castle* was so useful an introduction to England was that it was about the English encounter with Americans, and vice versa. It is in explaining England to the visiting American brothers, Neil and Simon —not to mention explaining their national peculiarities to herself—that Cassandra elaborates for us the differences between the two countries. Everything from the details of table manners (Neil at one point criticizes "the way you all hang onto your knives") to the nuances of vocabulary ("Americans say 'perfume' instead of 'scent'") is recorded by Cassandra. She becomes our investigating anthropologist, with the result that—as in early Hitchcock movies—the insularity of the English, scrutinized from within, becomes the Briton's own choicest subject. Nowhere in the book is this double vision more apparent than in the scene where Neil tries to help Cassandra imagine the American landscape:

> We shut our eyes and concentrated hard. I think the pictures I saw were just my imaginings of what he had described, but I did get the strangest feeling of space and freedom—so that when I opened my eyes, the fields and hedges and even the sky seemed so close that they were almost pressing on me. Neil looked quite startled when I told him; he said that was how he felt most of the time in England.

It would be foolish of me, I suppose, to trace my lifelong love of Henry James and his Anglo-American encounters back to this single passage. It is a fruitful subject, the fun-

house-mirror relationship between the two cousinly cul-
tures, and I would have come upon it elsewhere if not here.
But I do remember coming upon it here, and that passage is
one of the half-dozen or so that stayed with me, in almost
perfect form, over the thirty-some-year interval between my
last reading of the book and this one. That an American man
could help you understand what it meant to be an English
woman—or, in my case, that a British man could clarify for
me my Americanness—was a discovery I was to make repeatedly, in books and in life.

I have said that the weakest scenes in *Lucky Jim* are the
love scenes, and in this way too Smith's novel is the opposite
of Amis's, for *I Capture the Castle* is very good on how it feels
to fall in love—not just with a person, but also with a book,
a place, a piece of music. Few books are persuasively able to
describe happiness, but this, for me, remains one of those
few. "I took pleasure in moving, both in the physical effort
and in the touch of the air—it was most queer how the air
did seem to touch me, even when it was very still," Cassandra tells us about a particularly happy day she spent alone at
the castle. The vividness of that self-sufficient joy, the way it
is a physical feeling as well as a psychological one, strikes a
deep chord. And so does the rest of her description:

> All day long I had a sense of great ease and spaciousness. And
> my happiness had a strange, remembered quality as though I
> had lived it before . . . It seems to me now that the whole day
> was like an avenue leading to a home I had loved once but
> forgotten, the memory of which was coming back so dimly, so
> gradually, as I wandered along, that only when my home at
> last lay before me did I cry: "Now I know why I have been
> happy!"

That desire to pin down the fleeting moment—to view
it as if in retrospect, as already a "remembered" past—and
that sense of recognition which colors even the newest

beloved experience: these are still, for me, thrillingly accurate perceptions about the nature of happiness. To what extent had I even *had* such experiences when I was thirteen? I don't know; my memory refuses to give up the answer. What I do know is that I have had them many times since, in detail, down to the specific metaphor of the avenue leading to the faintly remembered home. In fact, this image has such emotional resonance for me that even a real walk down a real avenue of trees can evoke, as if by figurative reference, a sense of impending joy.

Lucky Jim and *I Capture the Castle* are both, in their own ways, romances. But their ways are a study in contrasts. Amis's novel is a romance of closure: all comes miraculously right in the end, with all the little plot strands tied neatly together, so that the characters—having no other job to perform—essentially cease to exist the minute you have turned the last page. Smith's novel is a romance of openendedness, in which the highest value is unfulfilled possibility. This feeling so permeates the book that I even dreamed about its characters, in their imaginarily continuing lives, the night after I finished rereading it.

And yet the opposite is also true. *Lucky Jim* is a novel in which—precisely because luck is the guiding factor—anything can happen to anyone. A fate lands on you, and you accept it: happily if it is a good one, unhappily if not. "To write things down as luck wasn't the same as writing them off as nonexistent or in some way beneath consideration," Jim realizes toward the end of the novel. "Christine was still nicer and prettier than Margaret, and all the deductions that could be drawn from that fact should be drawn: there was no end to the ways in which nice things are nicer than nasty ones." A certain ruthlessness can be heard in the tone here, which should come as no surprise, since luck often gives rise to ruthlessness, or vice versa.

In *I Capture the Castle,* fate is much more tied to character.

The character you are assigned (whether in life or in fiction) is certainly a matter of luck, at least in part; but if you believe that character influences outcomes, you are going to feel simultaneously more in control of your fate and more trapped by it than if you simply believe in luck. The possibilities available to you are limited, but that makes it even more important that you choose the right one. And this, in turn, means that you have to think about your own character in order to assist in the unfolding of your life.

When I was a small child, I had a picture book called *I'll Be You and You Be Me*. In one sequence, a little girl and her younger brother stand in front of a mirror, thinking about what they'll be when they grow up. "I think I'll grow up to be a ballerina," says the little girl. "I think I'll grow up to be a princess." As she says each sentence, the corresponding image appears in the mirror: a figure in toe shoes, a lady wearing a crown. In the final panel, the little boy, who has been silent until then, says, "I think I'll grow up to be a steamshovel"—and in the mirror we see a large steamshovel menacing the princess.

As a small child, an adolescent, and even a youngish adult, I thought I would grow up to be a steamshovel. Just as the little boy did not feel confined to his species, I did not feel confined by any of my physical or historical characteristics. I did not, I think, even see myself from the outside, as a specific person with particular strengths, needs, and limitations. I felt every possibility was open to me. And that sense of infinite expectation was what *Lucky Jim* so cleverly chimed in with.

At that age, I could easily take Dixon's side against the unattractive Margaret and in favor of the breasty Christine, because I did not even view myself as especially female. I find that I still dislike Margaret (it would be impossible not to), but the ease of it has disappeared. My distaste for her is mingled now with an unquellable resentment at Jim Dixon's notion that Margaret's annoying character "probably derived, as he'd thought before, from the anterior bad luck of being sexually unattractive," whereas Christine's nicer character "resulted, in part at any rate, from having been lucky with her face and figure." I want to cry out: And who is *he* to talk? Does he think *he's* such a big prize?

Apparently, sometime in the last thirty years, I have come to feel identified by sex. And by this I do not just mean gender; it is not just that I can now see, looking in the mirror, that I am a woman rather than a steamshovel. It is also that I now feel defined by the people I have loved and the ways I have loved them. I have been limited by those loves, but also created by them. I can see in myself the history of my big and little passions, and the choices I continue to make spring from a character shaped by those feelings. I don't mean this as a pre-feminist capitulation to some "Love is a woman's life" position. My sense of being a passionate, impassioned character inflects not just my relations with other people but also my relationship with my work.

This perception, it seems to me, lies at the core of *I Capture the Castle*. By the end of the novel, we sense that Cassandra's choices—of who she wants to be, and whom she wants to be it *with*—are unavoidably interdependent. Having fallen in love with Simon, she can no longer be the entirely free agent she was at the book's beginning; but her love does not require her to choose him at the expense of something else she holds dear (truth, say, or her writing, which may come to the same thing).

Perhaps what I am saying is that, whereas I once thought I could grow up to be Jim Dixon, I now see I have turned out much more like Cassandra Mortmain. This is not simply a matter of being a woman. Many men of my acquaintance have turned out to be more like Cassandra Mortmain (or Isabel Archer, or Proust's Marcel, or Paul Morel) than they have like Jim Dixon (or Tom Jones, or Becky Sharp, or Augie

March). Falling on their feet through luck alone would not be enough for them; they want to know why they got there, and how. They view their lives not as an achieved position but as a continuing story. And if you see your life in this way, that continuity will be with other people as well as with your own history—or rather, it will not be possible to separate the two, because the character through which you shape your unfolding story, though it may have a consistent core, is constantly altered by the people who have come to occupy that story with you.

And some of them may well be fictional people. I don't mean to suggest that fiction and reality are indifferentiable; only a lunatic would imagine she had actually *met* Jim Dixon or Cassandra Mortmain. But if you are someone who cares deeply about reading, you may find that you respond to the important books in your life, and especially to those early in your life, very much as you do to actual people. Sometimes you like them because they reflect exactly what you are at the moment you first encounter them, and sometimes you like them for the opposite reason—because they touch something in you that is hidden, or because they forecast something that you will be but aren't yet. Do the books actually cause you to develop in this direction, or are they simply markers along an existing route? The question piques and tantalizes but, like all questions about how we turned into who we turned into, it has no firm answer.

RECOLLECTED IN
TRANQUILLITY

I WAS NEVER very fond of
either Pope or Wordsworth. When I first read them, as an undergraduate, they figured in my life as merely assigned reading, and not particularly welcome assignments at that. Though I admired the occasionally witty turn of phrase, Alexander Pope struck me overall as too rigid, too arch, too artificial, too emotionless. William Wordsworth erred in the opposite direction: prolix, vague, sentimentally nostalgic, and maudlin when not excessively exuberant. These were the respective flaws, I felt, of "neoclassical" and "romantic" poetry (the academic rubrics under which I had been introduced to the two poets), and I had no desire to read further in either category.

The poets I liked best at the time were Emily Dickinson and Gerard Manley Hopkins. I still like them. They permanently shaped my idea of what good poetry is, so that when I later encountered John Donne, Wilfred Owen, Randall Jarrell, and Thom Gunn, my instant attachment to their poems owed something to that earlier affinity. What *was* the affinity, exactly? Not religious feeling—I lack it entirely, and so does Thom Gunn. Not scalpel-like precision of language (Jarrell and Owen can be faulted there), nor its seeming opposite, the overtones of everyday speech: Donne's and Hopkins's intense compression can hardly be said to resemble talk. Not, or not quite, the ability to render pain in words. I might call what they have in common "forcefulness." The feeling of the poems is vitally, rhythmically present on the surface, even as something more mixed and difficult—in the way of logic, grammar, metaphor, allusion—is going on underneath. You can love these poets the first time you read them, even if you are young and inexperienced, and that accessibility has nothing to do with either simplicity or complexity. It has to do with how deeply they can burrow under your skin.

What this has meant, in my case, is that I can never get sufficient distance to reread my earlier favorites. Particularly if I have memorized the poem, as I did with Dickinson's "I heard a fly buzz when I died" and Hopkins's "Margaret, are you grieving over Goldengrove unleaving," the initial reading and the successive rereadings fit as neatly over one another as congruent triangles, so that the uppermost one disappears into those beneath it. I can get older, and read more about poetry, and acquire unrelated tastes in all sorts of fields, and suffer in different ways, and experience new kinds of happiness, all of which *should* change me as a reader; and yet when I look at or hear one of those old poems again I am carried back to the exact same pleasure I felt at the beginning—mainly by the sound alone (if the sound of meaningful words can ever be said to be "alone"). Since I understood these poems, at some level, the first time I read them, I don't need to change my relation to them as time passes. Need aside, I *can't*.

The opposite is true of Pope and Wordsworth. I still don't

love them, and I doubt I ever will. But a recent rereading of Pope's "Epistle IV" in the Moral Essays and Wordsworth's Immortality Ode has convinced me that I hadn't a clue what those poems were about when I read them the first time. They meant nothing to my undergraduate self, who, balked by their apparent impenetrability, constructed meanings to substitute for those she couldn't find, thus obscuring the poems with the shadow of her own limitations. Yet now these two poems seem startlingly clear—so clear that, in retrospect, I find it hard to understand how I could so willfully have misunderstood them.

I came back to Pope's "Epistle IV: To Richard Boyle, Earl of Burlington" through gardening. I think I got to it by way of Michael Pollan's lovely book *Second Nature,* but no matter: the point is that I would not have been reading the Pollan (or anything else about gardening) if I had not lately become a gardener myself.

Some people use the word "gardener" as if it were like Painter or Sculptor or Poet, implying a degree of accomplishment and professionalism that might warrant using the term in the occupation space on one's tax return. I do not mean I became a gardener in that respect; my use of the word is strictly lower-case. But I did experience a transformation of sorts. For forty-four years, I paid no attention whatsoever to anything that was growing outside the houses I lived in (except under duress, as a child, when I was occasionally forced to help weed the yard). And then, in 1996, my husband and child and I moved into a house with a beautiful garden, and I adopted it as my own. Homeownership no doubt played a part, this being the first piece of real estate that I had ever been instrumental in buying. My love for the house as a piece of architecture helped, too: I felt that the wonderful old Victorian deserved its charming setting, and I meant to keep it up. But one cannot discount the mere passage of time as a factor. I had reached the age when patience, willingness to compromise, and tolerance of the unexpected—the great lessons of gardening—were qualities I could at long last begin to acquire.

Most of what I learned about gardening I learned from the garden itself. My predecessor had been a woman of excellent taste, with an eye for attractive combinations and pleasing variations, and I felt a caretaker's responsibility to perpetuate her work. For the first year, I pulled up almost nothing that was not a verifiable weed. I let all four seasons pass, in order to see what she had been growing during each, and though I added flowers and lettuces and herbs and vines to the existing pattern, I confined my subtracting energies to careful pruning. By the second year, I had begun to read about gardens and talk over possible choices with gardening friends; I had also become a regular at Berkeley Horticultural Nursery, the hub of local gardening. Emboldened by my new knowledge, I ripped out a woebegone rose bush and replaced it with a Madame Grange clematis, added a rock garden and ornamental grasses, planted fuchsias and abutilons and lilies and hostas where none had grown before, and eventually designed and set out a whole shade garden, complete with ferns and mosses. Through all of this, however, I left the garden's structure intact. The basic landmarks I had inherited—an old brick path, a towering redwood, some smaller trees (apple, date palm, magnolia, Japanese maple), a partially enclosing eight-foot laurel hedge, an adjoining natural-wood picket fence, and a profusion of purple-spiked Mexican sage, silver artemisia, and orange-flowered clivia—are all still in place, and I like to think that despite the numerous changes I've made, the previous owner would recognize what was once her garden.

In the course of this process, I had many small failures. Sometimes the problem was horticultural or botanical in origin: slugs ate all my verbenas, a fuchsia mite destroyed my earliest fuchsia, and a gardenia simply refused to blossom or even survive in my excessively clayey soil. But just as often the problem was aesthetic. I planted lilies where I thought the colors of the blooms would blend in well, but the five-foot vertical stalks looked silly against their low-growing neighbors. I let my predecessor's dahlia grow ferociously, only to discover belatedly that I hated both the ragged leaves and the grotesque, oversized blossoms. Charmed by the white calla lilies that had come with the garden, I planted hybrid versions in acid yellow and deep mauve; luckily these died of their own accord, before I had to face up to the egregiousness of my undeveloped taste.

The botanical errors were ones that pretty much had to be made—you don't really know what will grow in a particular place in a particular garden until you try it—but the aesthetic errors were, I now think, mainly due to my ignorance as a novice gardener. Eventually you learn to see in your mind's eye what something will look like when planted, and you learn to refrain from the severest lapses. This is true on the macro level of the garden as well as the micro. Nothing looks as ridiculous, I have noticed during my drives around Berkeley, as a tiny flower-bordered lawn introduced to the sidewalk by the sort of huge ornamental gate one might find at an English country house. There are many things I would like to have in my garden, in the abstract: a Japanese-style wooden entrance, arcade trellises covered with purple and white wisteria, a pond bordered with tall grasses, an Italian fountain, a symmetrically laid out herb garden, a gnarled Australian tea-tree, and so on. But all of them together, if you combined them in a single garden, would look random and excessive, and any *one* of them would look ludicrous in my small street-corner plot. A garden, I have learned, sets its own limits on what you can do with it, and good taste in gardening is at least partly a function of careful observation. You can only project your own ideas so far: beyond that, you need to be responsive to the demands of the place.

This, it turns out, was what Alexander Pope was saying in the fourth Epistle. "Consult the genius of the place in all," he urges in this poem about (among other things) garden design:

> To build, to plant, whatever you intend,
> To rear the Column or the Arch to bend,
> To swell the Terras, or to sink the Grot;
> In all, let Nature never be forgot.
> But treat the Goddess like a modest fair,
> Nor over-dress, nor leave her wholly bare;
> Let not each beauty ev'ry where be spy'd,
> Where half the skill is decently to hide.

Good advice, though it sounds a bit general on the surface. But when you have actually worked your own garden for several years, you understand precisely what Pope means about the delightfulness of secret corners and the need for restraint in planting. You have made exactly the mistakes he is criticizing here, so you can supply your own examples and counter-examples.

Pope has a feel for the specifics, too—specifics both of season and of foliage. His lines about the character who "sat delighted in the thick'ning shade / With annual joy the red'ning shoots to greet" could have been written from underneath my Japanese maple in April, when the shade *does* thicken as the once-bare tree leafs out with reddish shoots. Even the abbreviated present participle—"thick'ning," "red'ning"—has more than a rhythmic function here, for it imitates the paradoxical quality of spring's arrival, simultaneously ongoing and abrupt.

Needless to say, I missed all this on my first time through the poem. That an academically approved poem could actually be about gardening, and be filled with practical advice on the subject, was beyond my ken. So I made it instead into some kind of abstract rant about Taste and Hypocrisy. I know this, unfortunately, because in my edition of Pope these pages are filled with my youthful and never-less-than-idiotic marginalia. "Myth" and "live statue," the pencil scribbles madly, next to a line that quite obviously refers to a fountain in the shape of Cupid. "Hypocrisy–ignorance," "majesty a nuisance," "false religiosity," I maunder on, getting further and further afield. The sound of myself hopelessly flailing around carries clearly across the distance of more than twenty-five years. "Theme," I note in desperation when I come across a pithy comment. But do I really have any idea what that means? Evidently not, for I have written it next to a couplet that is sufficiently straightforward to require no commentary whatsoever:

> Something there is more needful than Expence,
> And something previous ev'n to Taste—'tis Sense.

I took this, in 1972, as an artistic dictum, a high-flown theory about creation, whereas now I can see that Pope is simply warning us against that oversized ornamental entrance— hoping to insure that we do not (as he puts it) "Turn Arcs of Triumph to a Garden-gate."

Perhaps my most embarrassing marginal note is to be found near the lines

> Spontaneous beauties all around advance,
> Start ev'n from Difficulty, strike from Chance;
> Nature shall join you, Time shall make it grow
> A work to wonder at . . .

Next to this I've scribbled, "Useful things of the past now seem elegant." Well, no, Wendy. This is *not* a disquisition about decorative antiquities. "Time shall make it grow" is a literal description of how a garden works, maturing and changing and enhancing itself as the years pass, not necessarily in the manner envisaged by the gardener. That's why "spontaneous" and "chance" (and even "difficulty"—all those failed plantings!) are such crucial gardening words.

The flower seeds that get dropped by passing birds, the separate vines that twine together on the fence, the moss that fills in around the bricks or stepping-stones—these are the means through which nature and time together develop the garden in a way that cannot be imitated by the mere exercise of human will.

From this distance, I can also see how my blindness to Pope's subject matter contributed to my tone-deafness in regard to his poetry. I'm not saying that the Epistle to Burlington is a great poem, by the standards of Donne or Dickinson; I still agree with my earlier self in finding it chilly and artificial. But now it seems to me that the artificiality has an instructive function. The strict neoclassical verse stands in marked contrast to the inimitable, surprising landscapes Pope uses that verse to praise. When he criticizes the sort of over-designed garden where

> No pleasing Intricacies intervene,
> No artful wildness to perplex the scene;
> Grove nods at grove, each Alley has a brother,
> And half the platform just reflects the other

one can't help but hear this as literary self-criticism. The rows and rows of matching couplets in traditional Augustan verse are like the gardens Pope doesn't like: symmetrical, exact, unremittingly planned, completely under conscious human control. It's true that here, as elsewhere, he has tried to break out of the straitjacket, loosening the metrical pattern so that the first line of the quatrain is noticeably shorter than the others, while the third line starts with a strong downbeat rather than the expected iamb. But the effect is a bit like trying to add variation to a garden by planting one side of an arrow-straight walkway in red tulips and the other side in yellow; the broken symmetry will still come across as symmetry. Pope admires certain gardens precisely because they do something that poetry (at least, *his* poetry) cannot:

they break out of the patterns set for them, producing "spontaneous beauties" in a manner that "pleasingly confounds, / Surprizes, varies, and conceals the Bounds." If we are sadly aware of how tightly Pope is bound to his rhyme and meter, that can make us all the more sympathetic toward his manifest admiration—I would even say, his longing—for a more flexible kind of art.

Yet Pope's heroic couplets do share something with the gardens he praises: the fact that time can make them grow. It's not that the words on the page can alter by themselves, as plants and trees and flowers do. The lines of the poem must always stay the same. But the observer can change her point of observation, and this produces a new vista, a new sensation, a new understanding. What comes from this shift in perspective doesn't have to be a large or permanent understanding. The pleasures of the reread poem, like the pleasures of the garden, can be tiny and ephemeral and nonetheless matter deeply. The point, in both cases, is that they descend on one from the outside, like a gift. My will alone did not bring about an increased capacity to enjoy Pope's poem. It just came to me with the passage of time.

Luckily, I left no marginalia on Wordsworth's Ode, and in any case I doubt that I still have the copy I originally read. When I came back to the poem again, it was through Lionel Trilling's essay "The Immortality Ode," which I came across while reading *The Liberal Imagination*. A word on this. I had owned *The Liberal Imagination* for many years, and a penciled price of $2.40 on the inside cover of my 1976 Scribner's paperback suggests that it was old even when I bought it, but I had never, apparently, read it. I *thought* I had, because its author and title were so much a part of the academic air I breathed in my youth; Trilling's book had been valued by most of the people who taught me. But when I picked it up to reread it, I discovered it was practically all new to me.

And what a discovery it was. My first response was an almost paralyzing admiration: why had anyone bothered to write literary criticism after Lionel Trilling, when he had already said everything worth saying? And even when I calmed down a bit—enough to see that there were perhaps a few dark corners his wise clearsightedness had left unclarified—I remained filled with enormous respect for his enterprise. He was speaking about things that mattered in a voice which presumed his readership cared about such things, and the strength of that assurance, in the face of the four subsequent decades' experience to the contrary, powerfully bolstered me. This was literary criticism I could learn from.

About Wordsworth's "Ode: Intimations of Immortality from Recollections of Early Childhood" Trilling said many useful things, and then he sent me back to the poem itself, reproducing it in full at the end of his chapter. I have reread the poem many times in the months since then (for poetry is the form that most invites rereading, its density insuring that you will harvest new meanings at each return and its brevity making such returns manageable), but what I did first was to reread Trilling's essay. Fresh from the poem now, I was struck even more by the essay's truth, especially when Trilling was arguing against those who believed that the Immortality Ode was merely, or essentially, about Wordsworth's own poetry-writing. He was answering both the biographical critics of his own era and, presciently, the deconstructive theorists of mine when he said, "And it seems to me that those critics who made the Ode refer to some particular and unique experience of Wordsworth's and who make it relate only to poetical powers have forgotten their own lives and in consequence conceive the Ode to be a lesser thing than it really is, for it is not about poetry, it is about life."

The errors I made on my own first reading were not precisely those which Trilling was criticizing, for when I first read the Immortality Ode I knew too little about Wordsworth to hazard a biographical interpretation and I had lived too little to have forgotten my own life. All I could see was that Wordsworth harped incessantly on childhood. The poem, it seemed to me, was *about* childhood (when it was not about nature, a subject I found equally distasteful). At nineteen, I had only recently emerged from childhood myself, so I could not imagine why anyone would want to glorify it the way Wordsworth was doing: "A six years' Darling of a pigmy size . . . glorious in the might / Of heaven-born freedom," or, worse yet:

> Not in entire forgetfulness,
> And not in utter nakedness,
> But trailing clouds of glory do we come
> From God, who is our home:
> Heaven lies about us in our infancy!

Everything about this passage, from the transmigration-of-souls bit through the God-and-heaven references to the final exclamation point, was designed to get my rationalist goat.

And even now I find such moments in the poem hard to bear. Wordsworth's labored ecstasy is one of his least charming characteristics, and his religious feeling, unlike Hopkins's or Donne's, fails to communicate itself to an unbeliever. But now that I am over a decade older than Wordsworth was when he started this poem, I begin to understand what he meant by it. "Intimations of Immortality" is not a poem about childhood; if it were, it would not need "Recollections" in its title. It is a poem about middle age.

There is no point in telling this to undergraduates. The paradox of teaching Wordsworth is that he cannot be taught, for there are moments in the Immortality Ode that just can't be understood until you have been through something like them yourself. It may be rude and pedagogically unhelpful to say this; still, I think it is not only true but one of the great things about the poem. Contrary to my initial impressions, the Ode is not based on a lot of sappy generalizing about youth and age and inspiration and despair. It is, instead, a direct transcription of an experience, and until you have gone through it yourself, you cannot recognize the description's power. That we all do, if we live long enough, undergo that experience is part of what Trilling meant by castigating "those who have forgotten their own lives" and have therefore misread the poem.

> There was a time when meadow, grove, and stream,
> The earth, and every common sight,
>> To me did seem
>> Apparelled in celestial light,
> The glory and the freshness of a dream.
> It is not now as it has been of yore;
>> Turn wheresoe'er I may,
>> By night or day,
> The things which I have seen I now can see no more.

The whole emotional weight of this opening rests on the contrast of tenses. Preterite ("did seem") modulates into present perfect ("have seen"), and the two of them are set against the comparatively empty, negative present ("it is not," "can see no more"). The word "now" echoes through the stanza like a funeral bell, tolling twice in four lines. This is the essence of the elegiac: a heightened past envisioned from the standpoint of a diminished present.

When I first read the Immortality Ode, and for many years after, I felt that I inhabited an utterly continuous self. I was the same person I had always been. The memories and feelings of me-at-ten and me-at-twenty (and, later, me-at-thirty as well) all belonged to the same recognizable character. I possessed my past fully at each point, and each point was an element in the unbroken line that made up my life. Or so I thought. (We are talking about feeling here, not necessarily reality.) And then, not too long ago, all this changed. I began to see my younger self from a distance, as if she were another person. I started to wonder at her decisions, at why or how she had made them—decisions that led up to my being where and who I was now, that person with a husband and child, that woman who lived in a Victorian house with a well-kept garden. I began, in this sense, to reread my past.

And it seemed to me, when I looked at things in this way, that some kind of internal engine had begun to slow down. That is exactly how I thought of it: as a motor that each of us carries around inside us, moving us forward, fueling our actions and choices and desires. My motor had once run very fast, and that alone had preoccupied me. It was enough to keep me going on its own, without much outside stimulation. It tossed up ideas faster than I could consume them, furnishing me with more than enough to think about and write about. And then, sometime after I turned forty, I became aware (but suddenly, not at all gradually) that the little internal motor was no longer sufficient. Its beat had weakened, and it needed much more constant infusions from the outside—in the form of people, events, artworks, conversation, city life—to keep me going. The narcissism of youth had been replaced by the narcissism of middle age: I was more interested in the outside world, but I was also more interested in my own past, as a thing apart from myself but linked to myself.

> O joy! that in our embers
> Is something that doth live,
> That nature yet remembers
> What was so fugitive!
> The thought of our past years in me doth breed
> Perpetual benediction . . .

When Wordsworth uses the first-person plural here, that is neither an accident nor a mere rhetorical convention, as you can see when he shifts momentarily to the singular ("in *me* doth breed"). The experiences he describes belong to all of us; what he calls "celestial light" and what I am calling a little motor is born into everyone, not just poets (though poets may be the ones most likely to consider the effect of such experiences, and their affect). For Wordsworth, this initial radiance, this intimation of immortality, comes from the soul's connection with the infinite, with God:

> Our birth is but a sleep and a forgetting:
> The Soul that rises with us, our life's Star,
> Hath elsewhere its setting . . .

As for my motor, I couldn't begin to say where I think it comes from. But Wordsworth and I needn't agree on this point. It is enough that we both feel the internal spark was once there and is now gone, or at least faded, accessible only through recollection.

The effect of this realization—whether it makes you melancholy, or sardonic, or desperate, or thoughtful—depends in large part on your character. We do not all respond to this universal experience in the same way. Wordsworth became elegiac. Robert Musil became bitterly humorous, or so it would seem from a marvelous passage in *The Man Without Qualities*, where the main character remarks of a friend, "There is no second such example of inevitability as that offered by a gifted young man narrowing himself down into an ordinary man, not as the result of any blow of fate, but through a kind of pre-ordained shrinkage."

Something of this same sense of inevitability also appears in the Wordsworth poem, when he speaks about the child's role-playing:

> The little Actor cons another part;
> Filling from time to time his "humorous stage"
> With all the persons, down to palsied Age,

That Life brings with her in her equipage;
As if his whole vocation
Were endless imitation.

There is a thrilling vertiginousness to this passage, because it captures in one snapshot—or rather, in one brief sequence of home-movie film—both the child's game and the adult's take on that game. That is, Wordsworth is simultaneously referring to a real if imagined child (the "six years' Darling of a pigmy size" who inhabits this section of the poem) and setting up a much larger, more abstract allegory of human existence. And the whole pathos of the stanza, or at any rate a large part of it, comes from the way those two evocations fail to match up. What is a funny game for the child is a terrible truth for us; his fast-forward is our rewind, but with a difference, because hindsight actually alters the meaning of the events themselves.

The writer Jenny Diski, in a wonderful Diary piece published in the *London Review of Books*, talks about turning fifty and looking back on being nine. What gives her article a Wordsworthian twist is that she remembers being nine and trying, unsuccessfully, to imagine herself at fifty. "But the best I can do," she recalls in the voice of that younger self, "is to imagine someone who is not me, though not someone I know, being 50. She looks like an old lady . . . I can't connect me thinking about her with the fact that I will be her in 41 years' time." So Diski, at nine, does "the next best thing. I send a message out into the future, etch into my brain cells a memo to the other person, who will be me grown to 50, to remember this moment, this very moment, this actual second when I am nine, in bed, in the dark, trying to imagine being 50."

And now, at fifty, Jenny Diski receives the memo. "The vividness of her making a note to remember the moment when she is 50 is startling," says Diski, maintaining the third-person way of viewing her other self that she invented when she was nine. "But it's not a simple, direct link. I have the moment, but the person I connect with is someone whose future I know. I do not know the nine-year-old as she was then, at all; the one who had not yet experienced the life I led between her and me." The feeling of disconnected connection, of "having arrived at the unimaginable point she reached out towards," gives rise in Diski to exactly the feelings I got from the Wordsworth passage: "a sense of vertigo, something quite dizzying." This is the sensation that accompanies the deep shock of perceiving our own life's one-wayness—or, as Jenny Diski says about her younger self, "of recalling her message and being in a position—but not able—to answer it."

If I, on the verge of turning fifty, am drawn to moments like those in Diski's essay and Wordsworth's poem, it is not just because our "whole vocation" is "endless imitation." That is, I am not solely moved by seeing the recapitulation of my life in other lives, hearing their tale as also my tale, though this is naturally a part of what moves me. It is always good to have articulate company. But reassuring notions of universality and common ground seem singularly out of place here. For what I feel, reading their "recollections of early childhood," is the very specificity of memory's texture, and hence the deeper pathos inherent in the fact of separation: even *this* adult, the one person in the world who might be supposed to have a direct connection with his or her remembered childhood self, cannot cross that gap.

AN EDUCATION

W<small>E ALL</small>, back at Harvard in the early 1970s, thought we knew what to make of Henry Adams. Though he had attended Harvard College over a hundred years earlier, he was nonetheless viewed as a sort of elder-student figure, and his *Education of Henry Adams* was therefore seen as a source of helpful advice about how to emerge from that cloistered environment into something resembling a real life. We found his attitudes toward our collective alma mater amusingly satiric, so that we were pleased, for instance, when he gave the title "Failure" to his chapter about becoming an assistant professor of history at Harvard, and enchanted by his assertion that history couldn't be taught. (Little did we imagine that we ourselves, with our one-sided response to Adams's complicated ironies, were living proof of his claim.) We all knew about "The Dynamo and the Virgin," or thought we did, and the little phrase was duly tossed into innumerable term papers to give them added weight. We read the list of his famous contemporaries ("Phillips Brooks; Bret Harte; Henry James; H. H. Richardson; John La Farge . . .") and wondered which among our classmates would be the modern equivalents. We considered law school and then rejected it, because Adams had already tried it and found it wanting. We were charmed by his childhood assumption that having Presidents for a grandfather and a great-grandfather was the norm of New England life, and we were prepared to adopt this mode of thought as our own, even without the prerequisite ancestors.

I say "we all," but perhaps it was just a small circle of my friends; or possibly I was the only one. Still, it felt like a collective attitude. And I do remember reading aloud—or having read aloud to me by one of my roommates, a descendant of Adams's friend John La Farge—some of the bits that seemed most pertinent to our own condition. Besides, what does it matter if my memory has falsified reality? "This was the journey he remembered. The actual journey may have been quite different, but the actual journey has no interest for education. The memory was all that mattered."

Well, that's not actually true, and Henry Adams himself doesn't believe it for more than a second. This one second of credulity appears in an early chapter called "Washington," which describes Adams's childhood visit to that city, and I suspect the observation about memory and reality says much more about the twelve-year-old boy than about the man he was to grow into. Nowhere else in his five-hundred-page autobiography does Henry Adams attempt to weigh the relative values of the remembered and the actual; on the contrary, his whole enterprise is a repeated and insistent (if also ironic and pessimistic) effort to get at the truth. Eventually he even seizes on the idea of "triangulation" to describe the way in which he, a twentieth-century man, could examine the thirteenth century (in *Mont-Saint-Michel and Chartres*) and then use this historically informed perspective to reflect back on his own times. Triangulation implies a fixed point, a firm basis of historical observation, and that doesn't really match up with the notion that memory is all that matters.

But then, there is a lot about *The Education of Henry Adams* that doesn't match up. One of the chief things I failed to notice in 1972 was what a very *strange* book it is. Perhaps its role as an acknowledged classic fooled me—but no, I read Swift's *Tale of a Tub* at about the same time, and *its* strangeness was instantly apparent to me. I think my error about Adams had a little to do with inattentiveness and a great deal to do with what I needed from him at the time. I needed him to have answers for me, like a Ouija board or the *I Ching* (though I would have scorned the comparison: I was never an anti-rationalist, even in the throes of a Seventies youth). I needed him to sort the possibilities, help me choose a life, lend me his wisdom as a guide—in short, educate me in a practical way. I thought (but what kind of crazy blindness did this require?) that his world was sufficiently similar to mine that I could build on his experiences, whereas what he was really telling me, throughout the entire book, was that his world had changed so much in sixty years that he couldn't even build on his *own* experiences. I took his autobiography as a firm link to the past—a version of geological uniformity, to borrow his favorite analogy—whereas he constructed it around the idea of catastrophism, with its severe breaks and discontinuities.

And yet the ultimate irony (or let us say penultimate, since I will have to read this book again when I have reached the age Adams was when he wrote it) lies precisely in my present reaction to that disjunction. It is when he refers to violent change—to its inevitability, its fearfulness, and its sickening thrill—that I find Henry Adams speaking most directly to me now. He was not my contemporary then, when I was twenty; he had no power to advise me about my future. But he has become something closer to my contemporary now. And the reason for this is not just personal, but cultural, historical, even technological, if you will. I know exactly what the Dynamo is now: it is the high-speed, computerized, digitally rendered universe I presently inhabit. (I say "presently" as if the computer and its affiliated mechanisms might go away at any moment, but of course I don't really think they will, nor do I fully wish them to.) I am less sure about the Virgin, but I suspect that for me the Virgin is something like the Greek temple ruins at Paestum, or a painting by Piero della Francesca, or a novel by Henry James, or even the autobiography of Henry Adams. The Virgin, for me, is the human attempt to create something larger and more lasting than itself—the successful attempt, I mean.

Was Adams himself a religious man, or was his "Virgin" as far divorced from strict Christian theology as my own? With a writer as slippery as Adams (he would say "resistant" or "a student of multiplicity," his preferred terms for self-contradiction), it is always hard to tell. His most emphatic statement about God, for instance, comes in the context of his sister's sudden death from tetanus. After watching her die in agony, Adams decides that "the idea that any personal deity could find pleasure or profit in torturing a poor woman, by accident, with a fiendish cruelty known to man only in perverted or insane temperaments, could not be held for a moment. For pure blasphemy, it made atheism a comfort. God might be, as the Church said, a Substance, but he could not be a Person." At this moment of emotional and spiritual crisis (it comes in a chapter called "Chaos," which also marks the outbreak of the Franco-Prussian war in 1870), Adams's tone carries all its characteristic doublenesses. You can hear the wit combined with the sorrow, the effort at faith intermingled with the resistance to it, and—perhaps most typical of all—the completely personal response leading directly to and stemming directly from a question of vast, universal importance.

Even the connection with the Virgin is doubled here, because if his sister's death caused Adams to doubt God, his sister's existence was, in the first place, what predisposed him toward his eventual Mariology. "She was the first young woman he was ever intimate with—quick, sensitive, wilful or full of will, energetic, sympathetic and intelligent enough to supply a score of men with ideas—and he was delighted to give her the reins—and let her drive him where she would," he remarks of this same sister as a young married woman living in Italy. "It was his first experiment in giving the reins to a woman, and he was so much pleased with the results that he never wanted to take them back . . . no woman had ever driven him wrong; no man had ever driven him right." Toward the end of the book, he comes back to the same theme on a religious note: "the Church had been made by the woman chiefly as her protest against man. At times, the historian would have been almost willing to maintain that the man had overthrown the Church chiefly because it was feminine." Or, as Adams says in the famous "The Dynamo and the Virgin" chapter (which, incidentally, is *much* crazier than I remembered it being), "The Woman had once been supreme." His evidence for this, as a historian, comes from what he has seen "at the Louvre and at Chartres"; in his own era, the idea of the Virgin "survived only as art." So I suppose we are back at my Pieros and my James novels, after all.

Complicated as all this is, I have actually simplified and therefore belied Henry Adams's true attitude toward women. There is the overt praise, the evident sympathy, and then there is something else: darker, more hidden, more painful and difficult. He is gallant toward women but also distant from them. I didn't notice, when I first read this book, how often it presumes its reader to be a "young man." One could write this off to the parallelism of his dual project: *Mont-Saint-Michel and Chartres*, which covers the feminine thirteenth century, is ostensibly addressed to a collection of real and ideal nieces, whereas Adams's chronicle of his own masculine century would presumably be of greater interest to nephews. And then, it is *his* life he is presenting as the educational model, which he would naturally expect to serve more usefully for men. But this is to leave out, as Adams does leave out, the entire story of Clover Adams.

Even at twenty, I knew that Henry Adams had married a woman who eventually committed suicide, but I did not learn it by reading *The Education of Henry Adams,* from which all hints of Clover's existence have been scrupulously deleted. Was this brand of pain not educational, then? Perhaps not. In any case, the story is his to tell in his own way; I don't fault him, as an artist, for leaving it out. (Perhaps he assumed we would all know about it anyway, just as he assumed that the news of his own time—"Oliphant . . . disappeared in the way that all the world knows"—would remain known forever.) And Clover's suicide, once known by whatever means, does leave a detectable trace on the whole autobiography. The praise of Woman rings—not hollow, exactly, but guarded, ironic, double-edged. If God is not a benign "Person," neither is the Virgin, for she too can inflict torture "by accident," and "with a fiendish cruelty." Adams doesn't say any of this explicitly, but then he doesn't need to. We can fill in the gaps with our own knowledge.

That is perhaps the most remarkable thing about *The Education of Henry Adams:* its porousness, especially in conjunction with its sharpness, its hardness. (Once more, Adams's favored geological metaphor suggests itself.) The hardness and the sharpness come from the literary style, by which I mean both structure and voice. Every chapter in the autobiography has its own particular job to do—sometimes narratively historical, sometimes more contemplative and theoretical—and every sentence furthers, in multiple ways, that larger task. Adams's prose style is a highly wrought artifact: one can feel the hours a day he spent studying French at his desk in Paris (this at the age of sixty, when he already knew French for all practical purposes), and one can also feel that elegant, distant, sardonic language being converted to his own American uses. No sentence in this book is unnecessary, and no essential chapter is absent.

Yet the book is always described as unfinished. The editorial preface signed by Henry Cabot Lodge manages to suggest that the manuscript was left uncompleted at Henry Adams's death in 1918, and that a stroke in 1912 and the outbreak of war in 1914 had silenced him even before then. There are a few problems with this account, however, beginning with the fact that Adams himself wrote the preface in 1916, several years after his supposed silence began, and sent it to Lodge (complete with Lodge's initials) for inclusion with his autobiography in the event that someone might want to publish the book after his death. Both *Mont-Saint-Michel and Chartres* and *The Education of Henry Adams* were originally published in private editions only; Adams had both a palpable disdain for and a less explicit fear of general publication, and it was only under polite duress that he allowed the Society of Architects to issue a more public edition of *Chartres* in 1913. His ambivalence extended far enough for him to plan a similar fate for *The Education* when he would no longer be around to issue the polite denials.

Besides, one can hardly view a long-awaited death at eighty as the kind of "accident" that leaves a manuscript unfinished. In a letter to a friend written at the relatively sprightly age of seventy-one, Adams more honestly described his *Education* as "unfinished—and unfinishable." What makes it unfinishable, I suspect, is what I am calling its porousness: to succeed, it needs to have its author's views of history intermingled with and confirmed by those of its readers.

I don't think I would have perceived this fact so clearly if I had not happened to reread the book in the year 2000. If someone had asked me, any time in the past thirty years, the date of the Exposition that set off Henry Adams's "dynamo and virgin" ideas, I might well have remembered it was 1900, but then I would have thought: So what? It's just a nice round number that allows him to talk about the twentieth century, that's all. It is only now that I have lived through a change of century myself—a change of millennium, the pundits and advertisers kept insisting—that I see how discomforting the moment can be.

Like everyone else who endured the closing months of 1999, I recall being bombarded over the airwaves by spurious novelties and momentous opportunities of every kind; and when I was assured that the bulk of this onslaught would be over on January 1, I was irritable enough to ask, "After the millennium, will they stop running the dot-com commercials, too?" Those two transformations—the meaningless click of the calendar, and the huge technological change that has altered our work lives, our social lives, our financial lives, our intellectual and artistic lives—seemed merged into one. At the age of forty-seven I felt distinctly left behind, a remnant of the book-reading past. So when Henry Adams said that "looking back, fifty years later, at his own figure in 1854, and pondering on the needs of the twentieth century, he wondered whether, on the whole, the boy of 1854 stood nearer to the thought of 1904, or to that of the year 1," I knew exactly what he meant. I was a has-been, just like Henry Adams.

And yet not *just* like, for as he unnervingly pointed out in the chapter called "The Law of Acceleration":

At the rate of progress since 1800, every American who lived into the year 2000 would know how to control unlimited power. He would think in complexities unimaginable to an earlier mind. He would deal with problems altogether beyond the range of earlier society. To him the nineteenth century would stand on the same plane with the fourth—equally childlike—and he would only wonder how both of them, knowing so little, and so weak in force, should have done so much.

True as this is, it is also laden with irony, of a sort that never fails to bring me closer to Henry Adams even as he observes how history's acceleration is carrying me away from him.

I should add that the Adams I draw close to is probably not the *real* Henry Adams, the person himself, who during the last decades of his life wrote self-pityingly despairing, harshly conservative, and rather obsessively anti-Semitic letters to his friends. In *The Education,* all this has been transmuted into something much softer and more complicated (even the anti-Semitism, which comes off instead as a strange but not entirely unsympathetic tendency to bring up the Jews). The deepest irony of all, perhaps, is that this delicacy of language forges a connection between Adams and a posterity he thought he would hate. The tone of the autobiography is inviting, comradely, intimate—the very opposite of the sometimes fatuous public pronouncements that tended to invade his private correspondence.

What *The Education* does is to make you feel that if you are taking in Adams's double meanings, hearing the contradictory overtones or undertones to his sentences, then history must not have pushed you so far away from the nineteenth (or the fourth) century after all. Tangibles, in the form of the written word, are not the only things that survive. Something intangible, between the words, is also there, still potentially accessible, like the tune of a medieval *chanson* that has remained unsounded for many years, only waiting for its musical notation to be discovered so that it can be played aloud again. We, the readers, are the musicians in this case, and it is our reading that brings Adams's tunes to life. And if the tunes are pleasing, that is in part because of their antiphonal structure, their numerous internal oppositions. Among the contradictory truths yielded up by Adams's *Education* are his perceptions that the forces of new technology are to be feared but also embraced; that childhood certainties are both a haven and a trap; and that, though the accelerating future disconnects us from the past, the always available past is what enables us to conceive of the future.

Skillful as he was as a futurist (Adams predicted, for instance, that Russia and women would be the powers to be dealt with in the twentieth century), this is not the side of Henry Adams I find myself drawn to now. Rather, it is his personal consideration of his own past—his life viewed already *as* a past—that seems to me both most moving and most chilling. Granted, with Adams it is never possible to separate the vast historical forces from the individual protagonist's past. They are inextricably intertwined, partly by virtue of the fact that he is an Adams ("If the scene on the floor of the House, when the old President fell, struck the still simple-minded American public with a sensation unusually dramatic, its effect on a ten-year-old boy, whose boy-life was fading away with the life of his grandfather, could not be slight"), but also because he has made history—all history, even geological history—into something personal to him. In the chapter called "Darwinism," for example, he asks Sir Charles Lyell "to introduce him to the first vertebrate," and learns that "the first vertebrate was a very respectable fish, among the earliest of all fossils, which had lived, and whose bones were still reposing, under Adams's own favorite Abbey on Wenlock Edge."

Yet if he is connected to the distant past, he feels somehow disconnected from his own more recent one. "Henry Adams stopped his own education in 1871," he tells us in the chapter entitled "Twenty Years After,"

and began to apply it for practical uses, like his neighbors. At the end of twenty years, he found that he had finished, and could sum up the result . . . He had enjoyed his life amazingly, and would not have exchanged it for any other that came in his way . . . but for reasons that had nothing to do with education he was tired; his nervous energy ran low; and, like a horse that wears out, he quitted the race-course . . . Life had been cut in halves, and the old half had passed away, education and all, leaving no stock to graft on.

The chapter is dated 1892, the year Adams turned fifty-four.

"It was not a bad life—in fact, it was a very good life, one that I wouldn't have changed for anything. But that was part of the problem, part of the awareness. Once change had represented promise. Now it was merely threat . . . The world was *not* all before me; at least half of it was now behind." You can tell from the first-person narration, not to mention the bare-bones modern style, that this passage does not come from *The Education of Henry Adams,* but I think you can also hear how much the author has stolen from Adams's autobiographical stance. There is the world-weary tone of distance from one's own youthful energy, the simultaneous satisfaction and dissatisfaction with the life already led, and the rather gloomy, eminently midlife sense that very little of interest remains to be done. Who is this thieving memoirist? I am sorry to say that she is myself, and her only excuse is that she was completely unaware of the theft.

You have to realize that I did not once look at *The Education of Henry Adams*—did not even take it off the shelf, except to move it from one dwelling to another—for nearly thirty years. Before this past year, I had read it only once, and that time not very attentively. So I was shocked to discover how much I had unwittingly borrowed when I came to write my own precocious autobiography a couple of years ago. The plagiarism is evident as early as my title, *The Amateur* (one of his chapters is called "Dilettantism"); I was obviously trying to assume the gentleman-scholar manner to

which Adams was rightfully born. But the theft goes far
deeper than that. In my opening chapter I jokingly referred
to myself as "an eighteenth-century man of letters"; Adams,
with only slightly more seriousness, calls himself "an eighteenth-century American boy." Rereading *The Education*, I
find that Adams credits his alma mater with giving its grad-
uates the ability to speak in public ("Self-possession was the
strongest part of Harvard College . . . He was ready to stand
up before any audience in America or Europe, with nerves
rather steadier for the excitement"); in *The Amateur* I tell a
story about my freshman year which, if you examine it in
this light, turns out to have the identical point. Adams
showed off his education while discounting its existence. I, it
now seems to me, was doing the same thing.

I am not, of course, the first American autobiographer to
be influenced by Henry Adams. Norman Mailer makes the
debt explicit in his *Armies of the Night* (he even separates his
narrator from his history-making protagonist, "Norman
Mailer"); and part of what interposes itself now between my
first reading of *The Education of Henry Adams* and my latest
one is the scrim, as it were, of the Mailer book, which I have
read two or three times in the intervening decades. It's possible, in fact, that I stole Adams through Mailer rather than directly (though surely *some* of my borrowings are original). I
take it as further evidence of Henry Adams's porousness
that he can lend himself equally to Mailer's actively political,
humorously grandiose purposes and my more blushingly
modest ones. Despite its apparent rigor, it seems, the voice is
a flexible one, and can be pushed in either direction along its
spectrum of oppositions.

Awareness does not necessarily imply renunciation, and
even now that my theft has been driven home to me, I persist
in confusing my story with Adams's. I cannot read his criti-
cisms of academic society, for instance, without adopting
them as my own. When I first read *The Education of Henry*

Adams, I seemed more likely than not to become an academic. Now that the die has been firmly cast in favor of the negative, I can read with wry amusement a passage like this one:

> Several score of the best-educated, most agreeable, and personally the most sociable people in America united in Cambridge to make a social desert that would have starved a polar bear. The liveliest and most agreeable of men—James Russell Lowell, Francis J. Child, Louis Agassiz, his son Alexander, Gurney, John Fiske, William James and a dozen others, who would have made the joy of London or Paris—tried their best to break out and be like other men in Cambridge and Boston, but society called them professors, and professors they had to be.

I think even my dearest academic friends in Berkeley, if they thought about it for a moment, would have to recognize this portrait of our strangely unexciting little community.

The part of *The Education* that seemed most far away from me at the time I first read it—and seemed destined to remain that far away from me—was all the stuff about Washington politics. Not only did I and all my friends and acquaintances lack presidential grandparents; we had no interest at all in electoral politics. I had spent the summer of 1970 in Washington, working at the Office of Equal Opportunity's Legal Services division (all those capitalized words seem so quaintly of their period, now), and I hated the town with a passion that has barely abated in the years since. So it came as a shock to me, when my near contemporary Bill Clinton was elected to the White House, to find that close friends of mine were suddenly being translated to the spheres of power. First there was the President's chief economic adviser, a Berkeley professor who, early in our friendship, had lent me her maternity clothes; she got snapped up during the pre-Inaugural transition. Next came a medical friend, a San Franciscan who had won a Nobel Prize for his cancer research: he became director of the National Institutes of Health. Then there was the poet laureateship, which went for the first time to a Californian—a writer whose name had long adorned my magazine's masthead. At first this sort of thing was amusing. But as the Bay Area started to empty out, I began to resent Clinton's admiration for my friends. As Adams put it: "Suddenly Mr. McKinley entered the White House and laid his hand heavily on this special group. In a moment the whole nest so carefully constructed, was torn to pieces and scattered over the world. Adams found himself alone."

But that self-pitying note (if indeed that's what it is, and not a hidden form of self-congratulation) is rare in *The Education of Henry Adams*, and whenever it sounds, it does so with its own reversal at hand. Adams is never exactly cheerful, but he is always *interested*. He remains intrigued by the world that surrounds him even when he professes to be utterly left behind by it. And it is this largeness of view, rather than any petty biographical overlapping, that constitutes the truly valuable inheritance. We needn't have known Presidents or gone to Harvard to receive the Henry Adams legacy. It is ours by virtue of the fact that we succeed him in time.

As he, in a way, succeeds himself. The voice of *The Education* seems to come at times from beyond the grave. It sees Henry Adams's life span as a completed whole, as if this particular man were simply another of those vertebrate fossils lodged in their proper sediment. That the narrator himself happens to be the examined fossil doesn't, somehow, detract from the sense of persuasive distance; it only adds a certain sharp poignancy to the tone. As early as the second page of the autobiography, we find him writing as if it were all over:

> Probably no child, born in the year, held better cards than he. Whether life was an honest game of chance, or whether the

cards were marked and forced, he could not refuse to play his excellent hand. He could never make the usual plea of irresponsibility. He accepted the situation as though he had been a party to it, and under the same circumstances would do it again, the more readily for knowing the exact values. To his life as a whole he was a consenting, contracting party and partner from the moment he was born to the moment he died.

So we have reached the end already, even though we are just beginning. And yet this is not the end, for the paragraph contains a further, final sentence that cements the social contract: "Only with that understanding—as a consciously assenting member in full partnership with the society of his age—had his education an interest to himself or to others." We, the "others," are made part of the triangulation here, brought into relation with that two-sided self, the autobiographer and his subject, who jointly give our collective geometry its shape.

Resignation is too feeble a word for the attitude Adams conveys in this exemplary paragraph. He is a willing player in the game, and that conscious, conscientious willingness is crucial to his education—and to his *Education.* The book as a whole is finally neither hopeful nor despairing. It is contemplative, and in that sense bracing. When I was twenty I looked to it as a guide and found it wanting. Now I turn to it as a consolation, and it satisfies.

A YOUNG WOMAN'S
MISTAKES

T HIS IS a difficult chapter for
me to write—not because my own youthful mistakes were
so egregious (I hasten to dispel any lurid expectations un-
fairly aroused by the chapter title), but because I may be
making a mistake now. It is always unnerving to find oneself
incapable of appreciating an acknowledged masterpiece,
and it is generally foolish to confess that reaction in public.
Still, I have gotten used to this experience in small doses: I
have never liked James Joyce's *Ulysses*, for instance, and
have long been accustomed to defending that eccentric position. What makes me much more anxious is to find that I no
longer love a masterpiece I once adored. In such a case, I
begin to suspect myself rather than the book; if one of us has
diminished over time, it must surely be me. And yet my faith
in my own perceptions is so central to who I am and what I
do—my critic-self, in short, is so unshakable—that I can't
quite believe I'm wrong. So I am pulled in two directions at
once: on the one hand toward shame, doubt, and the effort to

avoid public humiliation; on the other hand toward curiosity, a spirit of scientific inquiry, and the desire to publish what I have learned even from a failed experiment.

If only one experiment had failed, I might have junked the effort and resolved to hide the evidence. But when two recent experiments came to similar unfortunate conclusions, it seemed to me that education (as Henry Adams might have said) was being offered. In other words, it was only when I found that both *Anna Karenina* and *Middlemarch* had failed to work their magic on me, this time around, that my diminished reaction took on a potential interest.

Anna Karenina is on just about everyone's list of books to reread, and I gladly embarked on it near the beginning of my project, hoping and indeed assuming that a quarter-century's absence would only strengthen my affection. But whereas I had loved the book in my early twenties, the response I had in my late forties was much more ambiguous. I was amazed to see the once-disdained Levin parts—the parts I had skimmed through rapidly, as I had the battle scenes of *War and Peace*, so as to get back to the engrossing love story—taking over the book; the chapters devoted to Levin and his love for Kitty, Levin and his land, Levin and his peasants, Levin and his religious feelings are fully half the book, it turns out, and to me, now, they are the far more interesting half. And I was equally amazed to see Anna herself dwindle from a tremendously romantic heroine, an idol of my youth, to a rather dislikable, idiosyncratically neurotic woman. I had once believed that I understood and even sanctioned all her passions, all her choices. I had mourned her suicide as the tragic ending of the novel. (That Tolstoy carried on for fifty more pages about Levin struck me as tedious and irrelevant, that first time.) Now she seemed more like a shallow, self-serving escapee from a Flaubert novel; even her death scene was more histrionic and less sad than I remembered it. This is not to say that I disliked *Anna Karen-*

ina. Not at all. The book was still a terrific pleasure to read, and I relished every second I spent with it. But it was not the life-transforming event it had been when I first read it.

I was sorry and a bit ashamed to feel this way, but there was nothing I could do about it, so I decided to leave *Anna Karenina* out of my book. It would leave a noticeable hole—I would have to say *something* to explain its absence—but I could keep my embarrassment to a minimum by not explaining too much. Then I reread *Middlemarch* and found myself having a remarkably similar experience: Lydgate had expanded over the course of three decades, while Dorothea had shrunk. And that's when I began to realize I had a problem—the good kind of problem, I hope, the kind that is susceptible to inquiry and analysis, perhaps even yielding a solution. Possibly it will sound more enticing if I call it a mystery, or a riddle. At any rate, the question that lies behind the problem or riddle, baldly put, is: Why am I now so unsympathetic to these two young women, Anna and Dorothea, whose fates once meant so much to me?

My relationship to George Eliot, I should point out, has always been more problematic than my relationship to Tolstoy. Tolstoy was just there, like a monument: huge, marmoreal, flawless. As a young person, I never believed you had to choose between Dostoyevsky and Tolstoy, as so many people insisted—I chose them both—but I certainly felt closer to Dostoyevsky, more immersed in his particular obsessions, whereas with Tolstoy I felt I was just having the natural reactions anyone would have: how could you not love *Anna Karenina* and *War and Peace*? If Dostoyevsky was like a treasured, peculiarly excessive friend (treasured in part *because* of his excesses), Tolstoy was like a brilliantly compelling movie actor, an image of human perfection— not someone you could own personally, but someone you couldn't help admiring from afar.

George Eliot was something else again: a schoolmarm, I would have said in my more antagonistic moments; a philosopher, I would have called her in my better moods (though still with a slight tone of disparagement). The first book of hers I read was *Adam Bede*, and I pretty much hated it. I remember the circumstances exactly. I was eighteen years old, traveling with my mother and sister in England, on practically my first trip abroad (not counting one summer I had spent on a kibbutz in Israel, which felt more like summer camp than like my idea of "abroad"). I must have picked up *Adam Bede* in a secondhand bookshop—possibly the same shop where my sister bought herself a complete set of Jane Austen—and I was reading it during the London portion of our trip. I complained bitterly about the novel to my companions ("She is definitely not Jane Austen. *Such* a moralizer!" was the gist of my critique), but I nonetheless kept reading it, eventually becoming so engrossed in the plot that I stayed home from a family walk on Hampstead Heath in order to see the story to its end. Still, a certain annoyance at the author's superior tone persisted, and it was not until over a year had passed that I ventured to try another George Eliot novel. This time, with slightly more assistance from literate friends, I picked *Middlemarch*.

Again, the surroundings of my first reading have stayed with me. It was the Thanksgiving break of my junior year in college, and I was visiting my father and stepmother at their house in Westchester County (a house they still occupy nearly thirty years later, though everyone else in their old neighborhood has since moved out or died). With brief interludes assigned to eating and sleeping, I lay for nearly three full days on the living room couch doing nothing but reading—it would be more accurate to say devouring, *inhaling* —the Eliot novel. My body was in late-twentieth-century Yorktown Heights, but the rest of me was in early-nineteenth-century Middlemarch.

I remember certain details perfectly: the opening comparison of Dorothea Brooke to St. Theresa; the physical description of Mr. Casaubon walking in his garden, "slowly receding with his hands behind him according to his habit, and his head bent forward"; even the exact metaphor George Eliot used when she conveyed Celia Brooke's distaste for her sister's middle-aged fiancé: "I am not sure that the greatest man of his age, if ever that solitary superlative existed, could escape these unfavourable reflections of himself in various small mirrors; and even Milton, looking for his portrait in a spoon, must submit to have the facial angle of a bumpkin." I was especially taken with that spoon image because my roommate Catherine and I had already arrived at an almost identical formulation when discussing one of my undergraduate suitors ("He looks like a reflection in a teaspoon" were our precise cruel words; we could send each other into fits of suppressed giggles simply by holding up a spoon in the college dining room), so when I encountered the phrase in George Eliot, I felt she was speaking our private language. I felt that way, in fact, about the book as a whole, and now it surprises me to discover how much of an intrusive authorial tone the novel has, since I absorbed it the first time as if it were spoken by my own inner voice.

Rereading *Middlemarch* after a break of thirty years was a bit like seeing a familiar figure reflected—well, not exactly in a spoon, but in a funhouse mirror. The features were all there, but the proportions had changed so violently as to create almost a new entity. I remembered the basic sequence of events in the Dorothea plot; what I did not remember was how early so much of it comes. The prospect of her marrying Mr. Casaubon has been introduced by Chapter Two; Will Ladislaw first appears in Chapter Nine, before the wedding even takes place; and Mr. Casaubon is dead by Chapter Forty-eight, leaving nearly forty chapters in which Dorothea and Will's union is lengthily and repeatedly deferred. Nor did I remember the number of plot turns in the novel that depend on melodramatic coincidence: the sudden, brief appearance in Middlemarch of Mr. Featherstone's illegitimate son and heir, Joshua Rigg; Rigg's tenuous connection (via his mother's marriage) to the raffish Mr. Raffles; and Raffles's old link to the pious banker Mr. Bulstrode, whereby Bulstrode and everything he stands for are eventually brought down. Now these developments strike me as weird Dickensian intrusions, strangely inappropriate to the psychological realism George Eliot is otherwise trying to establish, but then they merely figured as necessary mechanisms to propel the plot forward to the point where Mrs. Casaubon could at last become Mrs. Ladislaw.

That you could marry the wrong person the first time around, and would then have to rely on a huge pile of unlikely coincidences to be offered a second chance—this, I suppose, was the central message that I and my friends took from *Middlemarch* when we first read it. The very word "Casaubon" has been imbued with the idea of a faulty choice, so that when George Eliot says, on first introducing him, "The very name carried an impressiveness," we feel it to be true in a way she couldn't possibly have foreseen. Casaubon is a specter who has haunted not just generations of Dorothea-equivalents but also a large number of potential Casaubon-equivalents: that is, if you don't want to marry a dried-up old failure of a scholar, you also don't want to become one. Especially for academics, intellectuals, and writers of any serious kind, the effort to evade a Casaubon fate has become a sort of shadow principle, mostly unspoken but always there.

I myself was never in any danger of marrying a Casaubon, mainly because no Casaubon type would have had me. Looks and breeding aside, I lacked the qualities that made Dorothea most attractive to her first (perhaps even to her second) husband: a certain pious saintliness, a willingness to submerge herself for the benefit of a superior spouse, combined with a strong but untrained intelligence that channeled itself almost entirely into good works and hero worship. And as for my choosing the wrong husband—well, by the time I finally got around to marrying, the husband I married seemed so inevitably mine that the idea of "choice" barely seemed to enter into it. I have been fond of saying, over the decades since then, that I married the only person who ever wanted to marry me. It is only recently—while rereading *Middlemarch*, in fact—that I recalled my one earlier proposal, received during my freshman year of college and evidently treated with so little seriousness that I never counted it as a real possibility.

But this is hindsight. Perhaps, at the time I first read *Middlemarch*, I imagined that during a certain portion of one's life marriage proposals would pop up like exit signs on a high-speed freeway: when you reached a divide, you would have to choose quickly among the available options, and god help you if you chose the wrong one. I was, I remember, very obsessed with choices at that age. But the ones I recall clearly are things like "What career should I follow?" and "What city should I live in?" I don't remember viewing life partnerships as the same sort of choice. If my youthful love affairs were anything to go on, my acquisition of a spouse was more likely to resemble a chance event befalling me than any more considered procedure.

That, I suppose, is where *Anna Karenina* comes in. I was twenty-two the summer I read it, already the veteran of several unhappy relationships and just then in the midst of one which was eventually to prove even more painful than its predecessors. Perhaps I unconsciously equated passion with pain; I know I equated it with at least a certain degree of unavailability. For a decade of my life—a decade which began, roughly, with that summer and ended with my marriage—I

viewed the adulterous love affair as the quintessential romantic episode, and literature, from Shakespeare's *Antony
and Cleopatra* to Harold Pinter's *Betrayal,* seemed to back me
up on that. *Anna Karenina* fed right into that mode of
thought. "From the moment Anna loved Vronsky, he had re-
garded his own right over her as the one thing unassailable.
Her husband was simply a superfluous and tiresome person." When I was twenty-two—unmarried, a free agent, a
potential mistress—I read those lines straight.

Now, of course, I can see how critical Tolstoy was of Vronsky for thinking this way. One of Tolstoy's great gifts is to
make us pity Alexey Alexandrovitch Karenin, the stiff and
"tiresome" husband, as if his were one of the central tragedies in the book. When Karenin thinks Anna is dying after
she has given birth to Vronsky's child, he goes to her and, to
his surprise and "blissful" relief, finds himself tenderly forgiving her. This highly respected Petersburg official, this
stuffed shirt who has heretofore seemed to care only about
appearances and status and pride, is reduced to a quivering
bundle of emotion, and we in turn are moved by that. Even
the unimaginative Vronsky is moved:

> Tears stood out in his eyes, and the luminous, serene look in
> them impressed Vronsky.
>
> "This is my position: you can trample me in the mud,
> make me the laughing-stock of the world, I will not abandon
> her, and I will never utter a word of reproach to her," Alexey
> Alexandrovitch went on. "My duty is clearly marked for me; I
> ought to be with her, and I will be. If she wishes to see you, I
> will let you know, but now I suppose it would be better for
> you to go away."
>
> He got up, and sobs cut short his words.

This moment of complete forgiveness is just that—a moment. It cannot last, not only because Anna survives ("he
had overlooked the possibility that her repentance might be

sincere, and he might forgive her, and she might not die"), but also because the social order in which Karenin lives will not allow him to be governed by his heart alone. He may have reached a state "of perfect peace and inward harmony," but

> as time went on, he saw more and more distinctly that however natural the position now seemed to him, he would not long be allowed to remain in it . . . He felt that everyone was looking at him with inquiring wonder, that he was not understood, and that something was expected of him. Above all, he felt the instability and unnaturalness of his relations with his wife.

All this is very complicated, and I seem to have missed out on it completely my first time through the novel.

What I had also managed to obliterate, until I reread the book this time, was the wrenching nature of the scenes involving Seryozha, Anna and Karenin's son. If it is wrong to interpret the book entirely from the point of view of a twenty-two-year-old single woman, it is equally wrong to view it from the position of a forty-eight-year-old mother of a son. Still, since that is what I now am, I cannot entirely help it. (Like Karenin—like us all—I am not only trapped in my social role but also infused by it, changed by it, made into someone who is no longer a free agent.) And, as a mother, I find the last scene between Anna and Seryozha well-nigh unbearable: first his unspoken hope that his absent mother will miraculously reappear on his birthday, then his dreamlike happiness when she does appear at his bedside, and finally his terrible despair when she has to leave again. What makes his distress most harrowing to me is the way the child's suffering is intensified by his passionate sympathy for his mother:

> He understood that she was unhappy and loved him. He understood even what the nurse had whispered. He had caught

the words "always at nine o'clock," and he knew that this was said of his father, and that his father and mother could not meet . . . she was afraid of him and ashamed of something. He would have liked to put a question that might have set at rest this doubt, but he did not dare; he saw that she was miserable, and he felt for her . . . "There's no one better than you!" he cried in despair through his tears, and, clutching her by the shoulders, he began squeezing her with all his force to him, his arms trembling with the strain.

And Anna is not just an innocent, oblivious recipient of this feeling. Even before leaving Karenin's household, she has in some way counted on the lasting quality of Seryozha's childish love and empathy. "And can he ever join his father in punishing me? Is it possible he will not feel for me?" she thinks, looking into her son's eyes as she contemplates running off with Vronsky.

It would be stupid and reductive to say that *Anna Karenina* is ruined for me by the fact that Anna herself is a bad mother. On the contrary, the things I have noticed so particularly on this reading—the emotional richness attributed to the cuckolded husband, the pathos of the son's feeling for his mother—make it a better novel than the one I thought I was reading when I was twenty-two. Yet the book has loosened its grip on me. To sacrifice everything for a fleeting passion now seems a seriously wrongheaded idea. I expect more of Anna. I cannot take in that she is still in her early twenties; I irrationally want her to have lived through the intervening quarter-century with me, to have grown older and possibly wiser, to have learned what it takes to keep a marriage going.

And yet I feel, even as I say this, that some deeper resistance is at work in me. It is not, or not only, that I disapprove of Anna, but also that I fear her, or fear the side of her that once lived in me. Could I still be the sort of person who is willing to smash things up for the sake of a momentary if powerful feeling? Probably not; but I am not entirely proud of the change. Part of the problem lies in words like "wife," "mother," and "marriage," which, though I may want them to refer to my own very specific affections and commitments, inevitably ring with a tone of pursed-lip conventionality. Have I really become so wholly a wife and mother that I cannot empathize with a passionate escape? If so, I regret the loss.

The odd thing is that the real-life escapes taking place all around me, among my friends and acquaintances, do not arouse in me the animosity that Anna's fictional one does. Something about her unsuccessful attempt to make a new life for herself—perhaps, among other things, its lack of success—closes off my normal sources of sympathy. I am angry at her for all her choices, including the final decision to do away with herself. As she flings herself under the train, she is thinking only of herself and Vronsky ("I will punish him and escape from every one and from myself"), but I am thinking about Seryozha. We barely hear of him again, after that birthday night when Anna leaves him for the last time, but I can't forget his frantic despair. Is this a problem with the novel or its crowning achievement, that its minor characters can sometimes edge the major ones out of the spotlight, depending on who I am when I encounter them?

I am critical of Dorothea Brooke too, but in a different way. That is, my irritation with Dorothea is inseparable, at this point, from my irritation with George Eliot. I don't blame Tolstoy for Anna's choices, but I do blame George Eliot for Dorothea's; he stands, somehow, safely distant from his characters, whereas she seems willfully, personally involved with hers. This is partly a matter of language: Tolstoy comes to me through the screen of a translation (in this case, Constance Garnett's), while Eliot speaks to me in my own native tongue. But it is something more as well. George Eliot, as a perceiving I, is individually present on her pages in a way that the more elusive Tolstoy is not.

Often this is literally true. Where another nineteenth-century novelist might hide behind the conventions of impersonality or plurality, Eliot has no compunctions about making occasional first-person-singular appearances in her own narrative. "For my part I have some fellow-feeling with Dr. Sprague: one's self-satisfaction is an untaxed kind of property which it is very unpleasant to find depreciated," she says about one of Dr. Lydgate's rivals in the Middlemarch medical practice. What marks the intrusion as particularly hers is not just the pronoun but also the distinctive combination of accurate observation, clever metaphor, and slyly ironic wit. This is George Eliot's own voice; we hear it repeatedly throughout the novel, and this time through I derived the greatest pleasure not from my encounters with the characters themselves, but from the charm and intelligence of these philosophical asides.

The problem is, George Eliot the psychological philosopher is not always a help to George Eliot the novelist—and by "novelist" I mean someone who, like Milton's God, creates her characters and then lets them exercise their free will. The fact that the plot is predetermined does not obviate the possibility of personal choice, as God is fond of pointing out to Adam, Eve, Satan, and everyone else concerned in *that* plot; and George Eliot would probably make a similar argument about the independence of her fictional characters. She does, in fact, explicitly make it about Lydgate when she says that "character too is a process and an unfolding. The man was still in the making." But despite such protestations of authorial non-interference, we can sometimes see the glint of the puppeteer's strings, for Eliot can never let us forget that she knows more than her characters do.

Nowhere does this come across more clearly than in her

treatment of Rosamond Vincy, especially after she has become Rosamond Lydgate. Eliot is extremely critical, for instance, of Rosamond's daydreams about Will Ladislaw:

> In this way poor Rosamond's brain had been busy before
> Will's departure. He would have made, she thought, a much
> more suitable husband for her than she had found in Lydgate.
> No notion could have been falser than this, for Rosamond's
> discontent in her marriage was due to the conditions of mar-
> riage itself, to its demand for self-suppression and tolerance,
> and not to the nature of her husband; but the easy conception
> of an unreal Better had a sentimental charm which diverted
> her ennui.

First, this is not entirely fair. Rosamond and Tertius Lydgate are, it turns out, poorly matched, and her discovery of
this might well lead her to fantasize about Ladislaw, just as
Dorothea's discoveries about Casaubon's shortcomings
have led her in a similar (if more unconscious) direction. *We*
know that Lydgate is a much better man than Casaubon, and
we know that Ladislaw is in love with Dorothea, not Rosamond, but why should we expect Rosamond to see things
from our authorially assisted viewpoint? And then there's
the problem of Eliot's rigidly expressed opinions: "No notion could have been falser than this." If the tone strikes me
as especially irritating, it is perhaps because it reminds me so
much of my own; we are never less tolerant than when we
see our own flaws displaced onto another. But I, at least, confine my certitudes to nonfiction. The novel, George Eliot's
chosen vehicle, is a form in which one generally hopes for a
little give, a little free play. If we feel Eliot's strictures too palpably, we are likely to want to pull against them.

That, I think, explains my problem with Dorothea this
time. To the extent that I believe her to be as warm and intelligent as George Eliot insists she is, I don't really believe she
would have decided to marry Casaubon. She is headstrong,

it's true; but in my experience headstrong people are very good at assessing their own emotional needs and arranging things to get what they really want. They don't generally rush into situations that make them instantly miserable. (The misery, if it comes, will take some time to surface, as it does with Rosamond and Lydgate.) I feel that Dorothea is marrying Casaubon because George Eliot needs her to marry Casaubon for a certain point to be made—possibly a point that Eliot is scoring against her own youthful piety and idealism. Nor do I fully believe in the passionate connection between Dorothea and Will, unless I agree to take it on Eliot's assurance. Let me put it another way: I see nothing in their passion that guarantees the long-term happiness of their marriage, and in fact I never *get* to see the marriage working out on a daily basis; George Eliot simply attests to it in the Finale.

People who have doubts about the substantiality of Will Ladislaw (and there are many of us) sometimes say that Eliot was incapable of constructing a good male character. But what then do they make of Tertius Lydgate? He is not only the best male character in *Middlemarch:* he is, I would say, the novel's most interesting character of all. It was to his dilemmas, and not Dorothea's, that I found myself drawn this time, his virtues and flaws I believed in, his mistakes I most rued. Yet even Lydgate's plot is slightly marred, for me, by my feeling that George Eliot has inflicted it on him.

There is something very odd indeed about George Eliot's relationship to Lydgate. She loves and admires him, but she is also very angry at him. She deeply resents the fact that he is attracted to unintelligent women—or, as she puts it, "he held it one of the prettiest attitudes of the feminine mind to adore a man's pre-eminence without too precise a knowledge of what it consisted in." And so, to punish him for this, she unleashes on him her ultimate weapon, Rosamond, who "never showed any unbecoming knowledge, and was al-

ways that combination of correct sentiments, music, danc-
ing, drawing, elegant note-writing, private album for ex-
tracted verse, and perfect blond loveliness, which made the
irresistible woman for the doomed man of that date." I
would say this goes beyond ironic wit to something resembling cattiness. Would I say so if I didn't know that this
George was a woman—a woman, moreover, more famous
for her wisdom than for her looks, which were so far from
"perfect blond loveliness"? I can't say; I can't undo that
knowledge. I even sympathize with the position she takes
here, as gossip or social commentary—I too feel that way
about the Rosamonds of the world. I just can't forgive it in
fiction.

But who am I to criticize a lack of sympathy with foolish
young women? After all, I'm the one who seems to have arrived at the stage—the grumpy, resentful, middle-aged
stage—of being unable to identify with a young heroine's
mistakes. Or so I would have thought, if I hadn't also reread
The Portrait of a Lady.

If Anna and Dorothea have in some ways died on me, Isabel Archer has only recently come to life. She seems to me
now to be the perfect young heroine. As passionate and intelligent as Dorothea, as willing to take risks as Anna, she
mercifully lacks the former's rigid piety and the latter's shallow narcissism. Like Dorothea Brooke, she makes a terrible
mistake in choosing a husband, a mistake governed by im-
pulses as generous as Dorothea's own. But whereas Dorothea's mistake was made at the expense, the suppression, of
her passionate, sexual side—her Anna Karenina side, you
might say—Isabel's was made in accord with hers. She was
in love with Gilbert Osmond, for reasons no one else could
fathom, and she chose him knowingly, comparatively. She
thought he had something to offer her (shall we call it romance, or art, or Europe, or critical intelligence, or inde-

pendence from convention, or a sense of vocation?) that neither the American businessman, Caspar Goodwood, nor the
British nobleman, Lord Warburton, could give her. If she
was wrong about the man, she may still have been right
about the choice. That is, if I work my way back along the
chain of her reasoning, I cannot pinpoint the moment at
which she made a false turn. It's true that she trusted
Madame Merle, who had reason to deceive her about Osmond. But Isabel had no way of knowing that, and her decision, as a decision, can't be condemned on those grounds. (If
we blamed all our bad decisions on what our friends or ene-
mies had urged us to do or not do, we would hardly be able
to consider ourselves adults.) Isabel's best qualities—trust,
warmth, adventurousness, generosity, and a desire to do
something significant with her life—are what led her to
make the marriage she did. If that was a mistake, I wish we
could all make such courageous ones.

When I was Isabel Archer's age (or Anna's age, or Dorothea's age), I was surrounded by intelligent, ambitious, passionate young people—men as well as women—who were
all afraid of making a drastic mistake. We all thought that a
moment of choice would suddenly be offered us and we
would pick the wrong option. We feared the decision that
would seal our fate. So when we read novels like *Anna
Karenina* and *Middlemarch* and *The Portrait of a Lady*, we took
them as a dire admonishment: look before you leap. And
some of us looked so long we never leapt.

But Isabel Archer's fate is not the worst one James could
envisage. That position, I think, is reserved for the hero of
"The Beast in the Jungle" (another touchstone of my generation). John Marcher is the man who waits so long for his fate
to leap out at him that he has, finally, no fate at all—or
rather, his fate is to be "the man of his time, *the* man, to
whom nothing on earth was to have happened." Marcher,
Archer: I can't help feeling that James had some kind of com-

parison in mind here. And it's this comparison, this sense of what a life *without* risky decisions would look like, that I now bring to my consideration of Isabel's fate. Rereading *Middlemarch*, I feel that a young woman's foolish choices are being heartily condemned, and rereading *Anna Karenina*, I feel that they are being more subtly disparaged. But when I reread *The Portrait of a Lady* I feel something different. To choose a life by choosing another person is a very dangerous course of action, it is true, but to refrain from doing so out of fear of the consequences is more dangerous still. I didn't know, when I first met her, that this is what Isabel Archer was saying to me. It's only now that I no longer need her advice that I can hear it.

ALL KINDS OF MADNESS

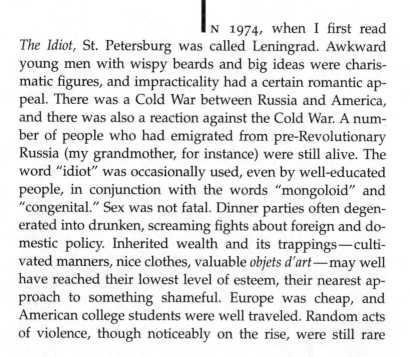

IN 1974, when I first read *The Idiot*, St. Petersburg was called Leningrad. Awkward young men with wispy beards and big ideas were charismatic figures, and impracticality had a certain romantic appeal. There was a Cold War between Russia and America, and there was also a reaction against the Cold War. A number of people who had emigrated from pre-Revolutionary Russia (my grandmother, for instance) were still alive. The word "idiot" was occasionally used, even by well-educated people, in conjunction with the words "mongoloid" and "congenital." Sex was not fatal. Dinner parties often degenerated into drunken, screaming fights about foreign and domestic policy. Inherited wealth and its trappings — cultivated manners, nice clothes, valuable *objets d'art* — may well have reached their lowest level of esteem, their nearest approach to something shameful. Europe was cheap, and American college students were well traveled. Random acts of violence, though noticeably on the rise, were still rare enough to cause a stir, and capital punishment in the United States had temporarily been suspended. Religion was an almost academic subject.

I cite these points about the era of my youth because they all bear some relation to Dostoyevsky's novel—to the lives of the characters in the novel, and also to the way the novel can be read, both now and a quarter-century ago. That I can use the word "both" in this fashion strikes me as uncanny. So much about the world in which I first read *The Idiot* has altered, and yet the novel itself seems to be about the present —my present, in which I am once again reading it—as much as it ever did. This is not timelessness, exactly, but a certain kind of prolonged timeliness: we are still, or again, inhabitants of the society Dostoyevsky perceived, and all our seemingly personal crises are acted out against that larger social background. But even to distinguish personal from social, smaller from larger, internal from external is to violate the subtlety and depth of *The Idiot*'s imagined reality. The beautiful Nastasya Filippovna, the pathetic General Ivolgin, the eccentric Mrs. Yepanchin, her high-strung daughter Aglaya, the dangerously singleminded Rogozhin, the dying nihilist Ippolit, the saintly Prince Myshkin himself —they are all a bit mad, in their own different ways, but their madness is less an individual trait than a reaction to the world that contains them. And if that world surrounds them, like something outside of their characters, it is also made up of those characters, collectively and singly.

All good novels turn life into language, but very few depend on the spoken word as heavily as Dostoyevsky's. What I failed to notice, more than twenty-five years ago, is the extent to which *The Idiot* is a nearly plotless series of conversations, like a William Gaddis novel but with quotation marks. "Talking heads," it would be called if it were on television; the phrase is usually used to denigrate, indicating tedium. And there is something like tedium—only stronger, fiercer, more unbearable and at the same time much more irresistible—built into Dostoyevsky's technique.

The characteristic emotion induced in us by a Dostoyevsky novel is one of painful frustration. Some lie is being put forth, some false accusation is being made, some verbal cruelty is being perpetrated, and the listener, the accused, the victim is receiving it in acquiescent, or at least unresisting, silence. Ever since I first read *Crime and Punishment* as an adolescent (I am thinking, now, of Sonia being berated by her drunken father), I have not been able to sit calmly through these scenes. They stimulate in me a physical impatience, a desperate need to put down the book and leap up into some brief, distracting activity. This is how I read all of Dostoyevsky's novels, and I consider it not their flaw but their virtue—a corollary of their feverish intensity. What surprises me is that I have not, in all these decades, outgrown my passionate involvement in that intensity. I can still bear it, just barely, which is the only way it could ever be borne.

The nervous anxiety that afflicts the reader of *The Idiot* is a pale reflection of the mood in which most of the characters dwell. What these overwrought people do, moment by moment and page by page, is to make scenes. They make scenes in the theatrical sense—scenes in which the dramatis personae may number anywhere from a cloistered duo to a chattering crowd, and in which the backdrop shifts from the Ivolgins' cramped rooms to Nastasya Filippovna's magnificent flat to Rogozhin's gloomy house to Lebedev's country cottage. And they also make scenes in the psychological sense. Repeatedly and exhaustingly, but not unremittingly—there is always a change, a cessation, a pause for recovery—Dostoyevsky's characters subject one another to hysterical denunciations, squirm-inducing confessions, freakish announcements, and various other gestures of despairing rebellion against the proprieties. They cannot all be certifiable lunatics, but they use whatever measure of lunacy they have to get away with—not murder, but the death of restraint.

(Did I even notice these scenes in 1974? If so, I certainly can't remember them. Perhaps they just struck me as relatively normal, or at least familiar, behavior. Dostoyevsky's speeches were longer than those I was used to hearing in real life or on TV or in the movies, but the extremity of emotion and the willingness to embarrass, offend, or even destroy were typical of what I saw around me, whether in Bergman's *Scenes from a Marriage* or late-night college bull sessions.)

Sometimes a scene in *The Idiot* begins with a slight departure from the norm, a bit of eccentricity that is still well within the bounds, and then slides rapidly to extremity. At Nastasya Filippovna's birthday party, for example, the "parlour game" of confessions, in which each person describes his worst sin, seems at first to be only titillatingly dangerous, still safely under control. But then Totsky—who, having robbed Nastasya of her innocence and respectability, now proposes to marry her off to the unwilling but mercenary Ganya Ivolgin—confesses some minor remissness in place of his unmentioned but well-known violation of Nastasya. This sends her over the hysterical edge, to the point where she throws a huge wad of cash into the fire and urges Ganya to pull it out. (That he calmly, silently refuses, despite his money-grubbing reputation, is what helps bring the scene to a quiet end.)

Or consider the evening at Lebedev's summer cottage in Pavlovsk, where the tubercular Ippolit, convinced that he's on the verge of death, insists on reading his "Explanation" to the assembled guests. Restrained at first by pity for his condition—or rather, by the sense that it would be socially becoming to show pity for his condition—his listeners end by raucously, cruelly egging him on toward suicide; and when Ippolit fails to kill himself because the gun misfires, they attack him for cowardice as well. Our own response to this scene is complicated by the fact that Ippolit is an extremely annoying, obviously double-dealing, insistently self-pitying young man, and, further, by the fact that his tryingly lengthy diatribe, while riddled with craziness, also contains some of the most luminous, intelligent, truthful observations in the novel. Much as we want to, we cannot separate the artist from the tale. Still, the wish to do so in this case is so overwhelming that we nearly drive ourselves crazy with the effort.

And where is the idiot in all this? What is his role in the craziness that surrounds him? Does he cause it or quell it? Well, both. (That word again: this novel is about being torn in two.)

Prince Myshkin (whose name rarely appears in the novel —he is almost always called simply "the prince") is not just the most memorable character in *The Idiot*; he is virtually the only thing I remembered clearly from my first reading. This is partly because he is at the center of just about every scene (or at its periphery: the two are sometimes hard to tell apart). As guest or host, witness or speaker, he is the character who acts as a catalyst. If others behave irregularly, it seems to be because his presence, his very nature, allows and even encourages them to do so. Until the end, when he recedes from us completely, locked away, speechless, returned to the distant state of idiocy from whence he came, his is the sensibility through which we perceive everything that happens.

And something of that sensibility—the innocent incomprehension, the need to piece things together after the fact— even invades the way we, as readers, take in the sentences of the novel. In its way of handing out information, *The Idiot* frequently makes idiots of us all: first we are given an inexplicable fact, and only later are we given its explanation. Interestingly, this is a strategy I was only able to perceive on this rereading, perhaps because I could only now read it slowly enough to take it in. The first time I read a novel, I tend to speed through it for plot and character; it generally takes at least a second, slower reading to make me fully aware of technique. But with Dostoyevsky, and especially with *The Idiot,* technique and character are intermingled, and slowness is essential to comprehension.

Consider, for example, the scene where the prince has a strange, inconclusive *tête-à-tête* with Aglaya Yepanchin (the girl he seems to love, and who seems to love him) and then leaves the house with her father, General Yepanchin. He bids goodbye to Aglaya and then, "as he and the general were leaving the house, he suddenly flushed crimson and clenched his right hand tightly." In the next three or four pages there are several more references to this clenched right hand, all equally illogical and unexpected. Finally, when the general leaves him on a streetcorner, "the prince looked round, crossed the road quickly, went close up to the lighted window of a house, unfolded a little scrap of paper, which he had been squeezing tightly in his right hand during his conversation with the general, and read it in the faint beam of light." The same faint beam illuminates the mystery for us: now, at last, we understand that Aglaya has surreptitiously given him a note during their parting handshake. It is not until the prince sees what he has in his hand that we are able to sort out the confusing impressions it has created, in us and in him.

Often these moments of sensory confusion, of delayed understanding, are associated with Aglaya. She wreaks havoc with the prince's sense and senses, rendering him even more tongue-tied, physically awkward, and idiotic than usual. But he does the same to her, because she can't understand the nature of the feelings he arouses in her. The whole summer society that surrounds her in Pavlovsk believes her to be engaged to the prince before she has even acknowledged to herself she's in love with him. How can she be in love with such a ridiculous figure? It humiliates her when people laugh at him, angers her when he lets them—itself a key to how she feels, though only her mother perceives this:

> "The idiot!" Aglaya suddenly whispered to herself.
>   "Good gracious! she can't be in love with a man like that," Mrs. Yepanchin muttered fiercely under her breath. "She hasn't gone off her head completely, has she?"

Now that I am Mrs. Yepanchin's age rather than Aglaya's, I understand exactly how unsuitable a husband the prince would be—not only for a genteelly raised young lady in nineteenth-century Russia, but for anyone, anywhere, of any period. But at twenty-two I shared Aglaya's passion completely, or rather, I went further than Aglaya. I loved the prince without embarrassment. I reveled in his violations of social codes, was charmed by his naive idealism, and found his awkward directness utterly winning. In many ways I still do; that aspect of *The Idiot* has remained unchanged for me. Prince Myshkin is still the most completely lovable character I have ever encountered in a book.

Given what I have come to know about Dostoyevsky's working methods, I am astonished at how precisely he achieved, in this respect, exactly what he set out to do. Here is an author who, by comparison with most of the novelists I care about, wrote by the seat of his pants. He would set out on a novel without any firm idea of where the story was going; often he would have part of it in print—as he did with *The Idiot*—before he even knew how he would end it. With the exception of *Crime and Punishment*, he was incapable of constructing a coherent, sequential story line. Character was everything to him, and yet a character could alter drastically from draft to draft: it wasn't until the eighth or ninth version of *The Idiot*, for instance, that he realized the hero should be a prince rather than a member of one of the generals' households.

But by the time he reached the beginning of that final draft, he knew exactly what he wanted his idiot to be. "The idea of the novel is an old and favorite one of mine, but such a hard one that for a long time I didn't dare to take it up, and if I have taken it up now, then absolutely because I was in a nearly desperate situation," Dostoyevsky wrote on January 1, 1868, to his dear niece Sofia Ivanova, to whom he dedicated *The Idiot.*

> The main idea of the novel is to portray a positively beautiful person. There's nothing more difficult than that in the whole world, and especially now. All the writers, and not just ours, but even all the European ones, who ever undertook the depiction of a *positively* beautiful person, always had to pass. Because it's a measureless task. The beautiful is an ideal, and the ideal—both ours and that of civilized Europe—is far from having been achieved. There's only one positively beautiful person in the world—Christ.

And then, a few lines later, Dostoyevsky interrupts his train of thought to say, "I'll just mention that of the beautiful people in Christian literature Don Quixote stands as the most complete. But he is only beautiful because he's ridiculous at the same time."

One can feel him, in this letter, working his way toward what was to be the crucial element in his powerfully effective strategy. The prince, too, is beautiful in part because of his ridiculousness, and his goodness is bearable to us only because he is at the same time so helplessly inept. Dostoyevsky is right when he says that there's nothing more difficult than creating a good Christ-like character—not so much because it's a "measureless task," I suspect, as because our tendency when faced with unadulterated goodness is to find it sappy, or self-righteous, or cloying. Bad characters are always more attractive than good ones, and Dostoyevsky was perhaps conscious of this when he planned, in an earlier draft, to model his hero on one of literature's greatest villains: "The idiot's character to be based on Iago, but he ends divinely." But he junked that plan, and all the other preliminary sketches of the idiot's path from sin to salvation, when he realized that the novel needed to start with an *already* good man. And at this point he evidently drew on the model of Don Quixote—a connection he confirmed, in the finished version of *The Idiot*, by having Aglaya hide a letter from the prince in her copy of Cervantes' novel.

What is it, exactly, that makes Prince Myshkin so appealing? As Ganya Ivolgin, his rival first for Nastasya and then for Aglaya, says with irritation, "How is it that you ('an idiot!' he added to himself) were taken into her confidence two hours after meeting her for the first time? . . . What made them like you?" People do like him, it's true; over and over, we see the other characters responding warmly to the prince, sometimes on first meeting him, sometimes after enduring terrible scenes in his company. In each case, the prince is able to do something unusual—say something with disarming frankness, or make an odd gesture of friendliness—that wins people over. But this would be a mere novelistic gimmick if it didn't also win *us* over. We can believe in the intensity and immediacy of other people's affection for him only because we like him so much ourselves.

Here he is when we first meet him, traveling by train to St. Petersburg in a compartment with two strangers who turn out to be Lebedev, the unctuous, utterly Dickensian civil servant who will later worm his way into every corner of the prince's life, and Rogozhin, the complicated figure who plays the role of Myshkin's satanic twin. (Forgive me for quoting at length from this scene, but I cannot adequately convey the prince's character without also showing how other people speak and behave in his presence.)

As the train pulls into the Petersburg station, Rogozhin turns to the prince. "'Prince,' he said, 'I'm sure I don't know why I've taken a fancy to you. Maybe it's because I've met you at such a time, but then' (he pointed to Lebedev) 'I met him too, and I've taken no fancy to him. Come and see me, Prince. I'll get those silly old gaiters off you. I'll put a fine marten fur-coat on you.'" And there are more offers as well: a new suit of clothes, ready cash, a visit to the beautiful Nastasya Filippovna, of whose diamond earrings, an impulsive gift from Rogozhin, they have just been speaking.

We get a brief, characteristic interruption by Lebedev—"Don't miss such a chance! Don't miss it!"—and then the prince responds with what we'll come to recognize as his typical directness:

> "I'll come with the greatest of pleasure," the prince said, getting up and holding out his hand courteously to Rogozhin, "and I thank you very much for liking me. I daresay I may even come today, if I can manage it. For I tell you frankly that I'd taken a great fancy to you myself, especially when you were telling me about those diamond earrings. I liked you before that too, though you have such a gloomy face. Thank you also for the clothes and the fur-coat you've promised me, for I'm afraid I shall need some clothes and a fur-coat soon. And I've scarcely any money on me at all now."

The most striking thing about the prince's tone here is his complete lack of embarrassment. He is not at all ashamed to admit his pleasure at being liked, nor is he humiliated by being poor; he is not even embarrassed to be accepting help from a stranger, but gives his thanks openly and easily, as if there were something natural about the transaction. This is not the proper way to accept a favor—one doesn't offer to come today "if I can manage it," as if one's own convenience were the only issue—but it is a far friendlier way of greeting generosity than, say, Lebedev's undoubted groveling would have been. It presumes an equality between the giver and the recipient that takes all the sting out of philanthropy.

When I first read this novel, I had thought very little about the nature of philanthropy. (I had probably, for that matter, thought very little about the nature of *money*, since most of what I needed had always been provided for me.) But in the decades since then it has become one of my preoccupations. This is not only because I worked briefly in the world of foundations, nor is it just that I run a little nonprofit magazine on behalf of which I have to beg for donations every year. The question of who should feel obliged to give money to whom—and when, and how much—has haunted or *should* have haunted most upper-middle-class denizens of America's late-twentieth-century cities. Poverty and need are daily evident to us as we stroll down our streets or look at our newspapers or attempt to ignore the circulars that arrive in our mailboxes. And the problem of responding to that need is not just financial but emotional. If you give a quarter or a dollar to the impoverished madwoman sitting on the corner with her bundled possessions and her embarrassed child, how do you keep from feeling either inadequate or superior? How do you define the relationship between yourself and the objects of your charity without sequestering yourself on some kind of moral pedestal?

This, I think, is part of the secret to the prince's endearing manner: he doesn't find charity discomforting, whether it is given or received by him. In fact, he almost seems unable to tell the difference. His unusual brand of courtesy is based on the presumption of equality—mediated, or softened, by a certain natural self-deprecation, an almost physical sense of his own awkward solitariness. This manner shows up even in his dealings with servants, as when he first visits the Yepanchins and is formally greeted by the general's personal attendant:

> "Will you please wait in the reception-room, sir, and leave your bundle here . . ."

"If you don't mind," said the prince, "I'd rather wait here with you. What am I going to do there alone by myself?"

Here he may seem to be simply childlike, naive, oblivious to the social conventions. But Myshkin's frank behavior is not always the result of his ignorance; sometimes, on the contrary, it stems directly from a special kind of sharp awareness. After a terrible scene at Lebedev's cottage in which a small group of nihilists tries to embarrass the prince into giving away some of his newfound wealth, one of the agitators, Keller, returns the next day to make a confused apology. After listening longer than politeness alone would demand, the prince gently asks him to explain the visit: "What did you expect of me . . . and why did you come to me with your confession?"

> "Of you? What did I expect? Well, for one thing, it is a pleasure to have a look at so simple-minded a man as you. It is a pleasure to sit down and have a talk with you. At least I know that I'm dealing with a most virtuous person, and secondly— secondly—"
>
> He stopped short and looked embarrassed.
>
> "You didn't by any chance want to borrow some money, did you?" the prince prompted him very gravely and simply, almost a little shyly.

Keller's response to this is astonishment—both real astonishment at the prince's acuity and feigned, fulsome astonishment at the way such a paragon of "simplicity and innocence" can nonetheless "pierce a fellow through and through, like an arrow, with such profound psychological insight!" That Keller's flattering observation is true does not make it any the less smarmy. Calculatedness—the desire to produce a certain effect or achieve a particular end—is the essential quality of most of the remarks made to or about the prince, and his own behavior, by comparison, comes off as deeply uncalculated. It is not just that Dostoyevsky needs the other characters' despicable qualities to showcase Myshkin's virtues; it is also that frankness and honesty might not *be* such virtues outside this social context.

Even within this context, the innocent desire to do good —to do good purely and excessively—can backfire. Whether this is because the fallen world cannot tolerate complete goodness or because unmoderated innocence contains its own brand of evil is not easy to say. Perhaps Dostoyevsky and I would disagree in our choice of conclusions, though his novel supports either one. Ippolit, who often seems both the craziest and the most perceptive character in the book, early on screams at Myshkin: "I hate you more than anyone and more than anything in the world—you jesuitical, treacly soul, you damned idiot, you philanthropic millionaire, you!" This strikes us, at the time, as insanely harsh (though "treacly" accurately conveys the cliff-edge on which Myshkin's goodness dangerously teeters). But the novel's end is no less harsh. How much ought we to blame the prince for the fates of the two women, Nastasya Filippovna and Aglaya Yepanchin, who both claim to love him? Incapable of sacrificing one to the other, he tries not to choose between them—with the result that Nastasya ends up dead at the hands of Rogozhin, Aglaya ends up immured in a lonely marriage to an impoverished adventurer, and the prince himself ends up back in a Swiss clinic, an "unhappy 'idiot'" whose doctor "hints at a complete breakdown of his patient's mental faculties."

I wonder how I could possibly have missed, in 1974, the novel's excessive focus on the word "idiot." I had not yet written any books myself—I had hardly written anything but term papers—so I didn't fully realize how much an author can put into a title. And "idiot," used in a pseudo-medical way to refer to those we sometimes called "the retarded," was still, though barely, a part of common parlance, so perhaps it was less visible to me then, less unnerving. But how could I have failed to notice the way it recurred every twenty or thirty pages in the novel, always in Prince Myshkin's presence—therefore an insult *to* him as well as a comment *on* him? How could I not have felt it as a repeated slap in the face?

This time through, I was conscious of all the different ways Dostoyevsky uses the word in the mouths of his characters. It has, first of all, the connotation of some kind of organic brain damage: simplemindedness, or retardation, or whatever would make a grown man seem mentally like a child. There is, as well, a suggestion of madness—feverish delirium or irrationality, that is, as opposed to mere slowness. The word seems, at times, to refer to epilepsy: the prince suffers from "fits," and the way he experiences the onset of a fit matches exactly the ecstatic transcendence Dostoyevsky reported feeling just before his own epileptic attacks. Since Myshkin is so obviously a Christlike figure, there are also strong overtones of the old Russian idea of a holy fool, a person who is closer to God than the rest of us precisely because of his innocent dimwittedness. And because Myshkin is socially awkward, a misfit within the comparatively sophisticated Petersburg society, he is also the novel's "village idiot," the fool in a less religious sense. Occasionally the word even seems to carry our modern connotation of absentminded or briefly unintelligent behavior. Contemplating a poor man's refusal to accept his charity, Myshkin thinks, "I should have waited and offered it to him to-morrow in private . . . for now it may not be possible to put it right! Yes, I am an idiot, a real idiot!" If anyone else had said this, it would certainly have our colloquial sense, but since it comes from the prince himself, the meanings are bound to be multiple.

The variability is purposeful: Dostoyevsky is obviously

playing, in this novel, on all the cultural and literary meanings we associate with a fool or an idiot. (Don Quixote, remember, was a madman too.) And Russian, as it happens, is a language particularly rich in words of this sort. There is a word for the feebleminded (*slaboumnyi*, in its transliterated version), and a word generally meaning fool (*durak*), and even a word with a special connotation of holy fool (*iurodivyi*). This last, *iurodivyi*, is the word Dostoyevsky often used in his notebooks when he was working up the character of Prince Myshkin, and it is the first word a Russian speaker would think of if you described a strangely naive, oddly virtuous man like the prince. But it is not the word Dostoyevsky used for the title of his novel. That word transliterates as *idiot*.

Derived from the Greek word for "a private person" (meaning a layman, a commoner, someone not in a public position), the word is essentially the same as the one used in English, French, Spanish, and Italian. And though *idiot* appears in a nineteenth-century Russian dictionary with all the meanings cited above (feebleminded, holy fool, and so on), it would sound to Russian ears, both then and now, like a distinctly foreign word—a word imported, perhaps, from Swiss clinics, where idiot characters and epileptic authors could receive the kind of treatment not available to them in Mother Russia. It is a word, in short, that is meant to stand out from its surroundings. Like the prince himself, it is both alien and familiar, partially understood and filled with multiple meanings. The strange thing is that, in the decades since my first reading of *The Idiot*, the English senses of that word have become less familiar, more of an oddity or an aberration—so that now, encountering it in the novel, I stand closer to the original Russian readers than I ever did before.

Something else has brought me closer to Dostoyevsky's language than I was when I first read *The Idiot*, and it is not, certainly, my own feeble Russian, dormant since high school language classes. In the 1990s a pair of translators, Richard Pevear and Larissa Volokhonsky, began producing new versions of Dostoyevsky's novels, and they were a revelation to me. *The Brothers Karamazov, Crime and Punishment, Notes from Underground,* and *Demons* had appeared by the end of the decade; and in particular *Demons* (their translation of what had formerly been *The Possessed*) gave me a whole new sense of how Dostoyevsky wrote fiction. Above all, it made me acutely aware of the Dostoyevskian narrator.

When I set out to reread *The Idiot* there was not yet a Pevear and Volokhonsky version, so I simply picked up the old Magarshack translation (as it made sense to do anyway, since that was the one I had originally read and still remembered). But even without a new translation, I could hear the narrator's voice as I never had before, thanks to the way I had been trained by *Demons. The Idiot's* narrator is not an easy fellow to pin down: he is not a named character, a specific member of the local community, as he is in *Demons.* But he is nonetheless a distinct presence, a recognizable voice, who steps before the curtain at times to address us directly and then retreats once again backstage. Mostly he occupies the position of a rather conventional, well-to-do Russian, a man of the world in these little Petersburg terms, who views the prince as an odd bird and tends to take the side of those in power. Summarizing the history of Totsky's exploitative relationship with Nastasya Filippovna, for instance, he enters entirely into Totsky's view, perceiving in Nastasya "something in the nature of romantic indignation, goodness only knows why and against whom, a sort of insatiable feeling of contempt that was completely unaccountable—in short, something highly ridiculous and inadmissible in good society, something that a decent man could only regard as a damned nuisance." If there is an edge of irony in this tone, it is so muted that it never threatens to become sarcasm.

His shining hour as a narrator occurs three-quarters of the way through the book, when he offers us a six-page discussion of the difference between happy ordinary people (those of "limited intelligence") and unhappy ordinary people (those who are "much cleverer," and who therefore aspire to an extraordinariness they know they don't possess). He refers by name to various "persons of our story" and assigns them to one category or the other, comparing them in passing to figures from Gogol. But even this doesn't set him up above the characters or put him on a separate plane of reality. We often, in real life, compare actual people to literary characters (I once compared Mario Savio to Prince Myshkin), so for Dostoyevsky's narrator to do this does not make his characters seem more fictional than he is. It simply makes him seem more intellectual—"much cleverer" than we had thought, perhaps.

As with all Dostoyevskian narrators, his view is both limited and inexplicably invasive. He describes to us, on occasion, things he couldn't possibly have witnessed: the meeting between the prince and Aglaya on the park bench, for example, or the horrific confrontation between Aglaya and Nastasya, or, most strikingly, the extremely intimate encounter between Myshkin and Rogozhin over Nastasya's dead body. It's not just that the narrator couldn't, as an individual, have been present at these events; it's that none of the participants (especially at the murder scene) could or would have told anybody exactly what happened there. So the narrator's claims to be operating on the basis of "rather vague rumours," or news conveyed to him through the local gossip network, simply don't hold up. Yet these are indeed his claims.

Toward the end of the novel, the narrator reinforces his detached position (cloaking himself, for extra protection, in the first-person plural) by informing his readers that "we feel we have to confine ourselves to a bare statement of facts, if possible, without any special explanations, and for a very simple reason: because we ourselves find it difficult in many instances to explain what took place. Such a statement on our part must appear very strange and obscure to the reader: how can we describe something of which we have no clear idea and no personal opinion?" And this know-nothing voice enters in again during the last few pages, where the narrator insists that all his facts and rumors about the characters now come from Aglaya's sometime suitor, the elegant Mr. Radomsky, who is apparently writing informative letters to Lebedev's daughter, Vera. Yet between these two assertions of distance comes the intimate, intense climax of the novel: the delicately, tenderly, frighteningly private meeting between the prince (Nastasya's fiancé) and Rogozhin (her murderer). The power of that scene, with Nastasya's inert form lying in the darkened background, stems largely from our sense that these two men are utterly unobserved: their encounter, their communion, is just between the two of them, completely invisible to and apart from the society that has otherwise surrounded them.

I cannot stress heavily enough how much this ending lacks any kind of postmodern, narrative-game-playing, tongue-in-cheek quality. The narrator's stance is contradictory, but his two roles—as social observer and as invisible scribe—mesh seamlessly. When we are aware of him, he is there, and when we do not need him, he ceases to exist. It is not a problem. It is not even a pointed strategy. It is simply of a piece with the rest of the novel, in which people are at once extremely private and inextricably caught in a social web. ("A private person," remember, is the root meaning of "idiot," but the prince, simply by virtue of *being* a prince, is the very opposite of what the Greeks meant by a private person.) We are all necessarily our public selves, caught in a particular world, and yet novels—especially Dostoyevsky's novels—find ways of releasing us, however momentarily, into something much more private and intimate.

And, among Dostoyevsky's novels, especially *The Idiot*.

Like its hero, it seems more porous than the other works, more open to everything, less fixed in its preassigned position. Each of the other novels has a plot that allows Dostoyevsky to carry on about one of his particular obsessions: murder (including capital punishment) in *Crime and Punishment*, religion in *The Brothers Karamazov*, misbehaving nihilists in *Demons*, and so on. But here, where there is no plot, there is room for all the obsessions to come rushing in, and the ongoing conversation takes them up each in turn. This, perhaps, is why the distanced, upsetting, inconclusive ending didn't bother me on my latest reading. My first time through the novel, I thought all that talk was leading somewhere; this time, I understood that it wasn't.

If age has brought with it the capacity to take in a work of literature more slowly, to savor its moments as they pass rather than hurrying to the ending, it has also given me a newfound ability to live with inconclusiveness. I no longer feel frustrated when novels don't end in clarity or firmness. On the contrary, I have begun to treasure works of fiction that possess a certain openendedness. Even as a young person I was being pushed in this direction by my affection for Henry James, but it is only lately that I have come to value the same quality in more recent novels—for instance, in the slender final works of Penelope Fitzgerald, which shaped me as a reader even as I was reading them for the first time. But even a wonderful novel like Fitzgerald's *The Beginning of Spring* (which, with its pre-Revolutionary Russian setting, has its own Dostoyevskian overtones) could not have trained me to appreciate authorial evasiveness if I had not yet been ready for it.

That readiness is partly a function of my own aging, I suppose, but it is also a necessary response to the history of my time. As Henry Adams pointed out, we appear to have been moving from Unity to Multiplicity ever since the twelfth century, and the hundred years that separate me from Adams only seem to confirm his theory that we are accelerating toward chaos. It makes sense, in such a time, that we should turn to the author of *The Idiot* for his thoughtful, touching contemplations of confusion and incomprehensibility. In relation to our own world, we are, after all, very much like Dostoyevsky's narrator—totally involved in the story, tuned in to all the local gossip, and yet finally limited in our capacity to perceive and understand what is going on with the people around us. Sancho Panza may marvel at the novelist's omniscience and George Eliot may take it as an authorial given, but Dostoyevsky knows better. It is his obdurate refusal of full knowledge, in the face of all our readerly demands for it, that renders him so unusually and renewably valuable to us.

A SMALL MASTERPIECE

MY FIRST READING of D. H.
Lawrence's collected short stories was like a sustained revelation, a single experience stretched out over time. I had
read one or two of them before, and of course I had read a
number of the novels: they were required reading in my college years, not because they appeared on any course lists,
but because we all thought they would tell us something
crucial about the relations between men and women. Still,
the novels all had blatant flaws (*Lady Chatterley's Lover*, as I
recall, was nearly all flaws), so I had learned to approach
Lawrence with something akin to wariness.

Yet even as I write this, I see that it conveys only a half-
truth. There was wariness, but there was also complete immersion. Lawrence is one of those writers who can be annoying, persuasive, overwhelming, and off-putting all at once.
He shimmers and shifts, depending in part on how far away
from him you are when you make the judgment. It is easy to
criticize him at a distance, but at close range he does things
no other writer can, and part of what he accomplishes is that

you are both with him and against him. You find yourself grappling with that intense, vehement narrator, who in turn seems engaged in a struggle to the death with his own characters—a struggle that may well force you out of his camp and into theirs, as if against his will. But "will" is a deeply ambiguous word in Lawrence: he is full of it himself, yet so suspicious of it that he trains us to resist. So the experience of reading Lawrence's novels has always been a complicated, conflicting one. Even those of us who cared for him enormously—and there were many of us, when I was young—learned to take what he could give us and decline the rest; there was always an excess, a remnant, an indigestible portion that stuck in our craw.

This was not, however, the mood in which I encountered the collected stories. I had moved to England by this time, and was living as an "affiliated student" (that is, a foreigner with a previously awarded bachelor's degree) at King's College, Cambridge. The college had housed me in the coldly modern Keynes Building, which was deemed appropriate for Americans because it had central heating and no charm. To escape from my minimalist room, and also because I had loads of free time (the Cambridge system required of its literature students little more than one or two individualized tutorials a week, and the work for them could be done in about five hours), I went to the King's College Library to read. One was allowed, I suppose, to check books out of the library and read them elsewhere, but that is not what I did. Instead, I chose a comfortable leather chair snuggled into a lamp-lit nook surrounded by bookshelves, and I sat in it and read. Did I choose the chair because it was near the D. H. Lawrence books, or did I choose the Lawrence stories because they happened to be on the shelves near the chair? I can't remember. All I know is that each day I would go to my chosen chair (it was never, in all my visits, occupied by anyone else), pull a volume of the short stories off the shelf, and continue reading where I had left off the day before.

I went through all three volumes in this way, story by story, not ravenously but savoringly. And they satisfied. I told everybody, then and for years afterward, that if the Lawrence of the novels was an irritant, an occasional embarrassment, the Lawrence of the stories was something else entirely: a master craftsman, a gem-polisher, a writer of great wit and cleverness and restraint.

The memory of this reading so inspired me—I mean the memory of the reading process itself, the lovely feeling of sinking into those books one by one—that when I got back to America I acquired the same three volumes for myself. I own them still, those three Viking Compass paperbacks: a matching set in terms of design, but each volume with a different two-toned color scheme, and each one priced at $1.45. They were used when I bought them, and inside two of the front covers are scribbled the owners' names. The pages, however, are clean, except for one set of helpful arrows in "The Blue Moccasins" indicating how to read two misprinted lines, which have mistakenly been placed at the bottom of page 831 but actually belong at the top. I can tell from the purple ink and the curve of the stroke that these are my own arrows, my past self telling my future self how to navigate the page. And what these arrows tell me, besides, is that I read some of the stories in this volume (the third and best volume) at least once after I came back to America. But as with so many unconsidered rereadings, that second one hasn't made a dent on my memory. All I can recall is the first, extremely powerful one.

So it is with surprise verging on amazement that I take up the three volumes again and find that many of the stories have turned—not to ash, exactly, but to something at once less glittering and less substantial than I thought they were. Lumps of coal instead of diamonds, I might say if I wanted to be harsh, but that wouldn't be true either; mica, perhaps, rather than coal (the geological metaphor suggested by the stories themselves, so many of which are about miners). It is some material, at any rate, that shines with frequent slivers of beauty or intelligence, but that fractures and flakes along its weakest lines.

Out of the whole batch there really is only one story that remains for me completely undiminished, and that story seems more miraculous than it ever did. The existence of "The Rocking-Horse Winner"—the very fact that there can *be* a story like "The Rocking-Horse Winner"—is enough to justify and excuse any number of flaws in the other stories. But I am shocked that I never noticed this discrepancy before. How could I read the whole three volumes, at the age of twenty-two, and find it a seamlessly pleasurable experience? How could I not sense the peaks and valleys in Lawrence's prose? How could I not recoil from his aggravating moments, which turn out to be so plentiful in these stories?

I have a number of explanations, and I suppose some of them would be considered extra-literary. But part of what I am trying to suggest, in writing a book that is both autobiographical and critical, is that even the extra-literary is literary. That is, to the extent that reading is life (not, god forbid, that life can be reduced to a "text," or that there is no difference between fact and fiction, or any other of those fashionable execrations; that's not what I'm talking about at all)—to the extent that what we read is an aspect of the life we have lived, and shapes our subsequent life, and becomes part of our memory of the past—to that extent, we should be willing to allow our personal and historical responses to flood in and out of the books we read. Our responses won't, after all, hurt the books; they won't change the essential, inalterable words on the page, or damage anyone else's readings of those books. So there's no harm in it. And there may be a great deal of benefit. But whether there's benefit or not, the bringing together of books and life is pretty much unavoidable, if you really want to immerse yourself in the pleasure of reading—and especially if you want to reread.

So what are the things, personal and historical, that in

1974 kept me from discerning the flaws in Lawrence's stories? Or (and this may be a more helpful way of putting it) what has happened since 1974, to me and to the world, to make me see problems where I once saw none? I am certainly not a more "critical" reader now, in the sense of being more likely to arrive at a negative judgment; if anything, I hope I've gradually become *less* negative since then, less willing to shut things out on the basis of a momentary dislike. (But I am, I'll admit, still pretty negative. One's essential character doesn't change all that much, and I wouldn't know how to be a critic if I lost the capacity to hate.) Besides, it may not be the case that I saw no problems then. Perhaps I saw and forgave them.

I am sure this is true, for instance, about Lawrence's gruesome opinions on the subject of men and women. In a vague sort of way, I had remembered that the novels were riddled with this stuff—you might say that we *came* to his novels for this stuff—whereas the stories were relatively free of it. But now I see that the stories too are filled with what I have called, in my notes, "the unbearable Lawrence." Here's an example:

> She was quite helpless. Her hands leapt, fluttered, and closed over his head, pressing it deeper into her belly, vibrating as she did so. And his arms tightened on her, his hands spread over her loins, warm as flame on her loveliness. It was intense anguish of bliss for her, and she lost consciousness.

That, in case you wondered, is a maidservant blissfully giving up her virginity to her soldier boyfriend in "The Thorn in the Flesh." The problem with this sort of thing is not just that it is badly written in itself ("*Actually* lost consciousness?" I want to say to DHL), but that it has been stolen, post-Lawrence, by the soft-porn industry. We read sentences like this and we think Harlequin Romance.

It's strange to think that the Lawrence who writes about

sex, the one I think of as the essential Lawrence, is also the unbearable Lawrence. He is bad on almost everything to do with the act of lovemaking (though he can occasionally be good on the subject of bodies, and on how men and women feel about their own and each other's). This has come as a great surprise to me. Less surprising, though unrecalled until this latest reading, are his opinions about the relative strengths of men and women, their complementary abilities and weaknesses. Here is Virginia, the thirty-two-year-old career woman in "Mother and Daughter":

> She had to earn her money, and earn it hard. She had to slog, and she had to concentrate . . . She had to do it all off her nerves. She hadn't the same sort of fighting power as a man. Where a man can summon his old Adam in him to fight through his work, a woman has to draw on her nerves, and on her nerves alone. For the old Eve in her will have nothing to do with such work. So that mental responsibility, mental concentration, mental slogging wear out a woman terribly, especially if she is head of a department, and not working *for* somebody.

I think the reason I didn't mind this kind of thing, when I was in my early twenties, was that I was so busy defending Lawrence from the people who *did* mind it, terribly. Feminism was in full flow by 1974 — a new, impatient, antagonistic feminism that didn't care what it knocked down, as long as it achieved its ends. It made no distinctions between bad offensive male writers and good offensive male writers; at its worst, it made no distinctions between male writers at all. This extreme form of feminism has largely disappeared — that is, it has retreated into academia and changed its name to Gender Studies, but its present impact on the world at large, the world of reading and living, is basically nil. And because it has lost its power, I don't need to set myself against it anymore; I can have opinions that are not dictated by its terms. (Because you are dictated to as much by what you oppose as by what you favor.) So I can see, finally, that some of the things the feminist critics said about Lawrence are undebatable. He is, truly, a bit of an idiot when he goes on in this vein.

But he is never *just* an idiot. Even the passages that most make me want to scream at him are filled with some quality I admire—desperate courage, maybe, or thwarted intimacy, or a reckless willingness to be wrong. Easy as he is to mock, Lawrence is never dismissible. We may hate some of what he has to say about men and women, but there is nobody else who is even trying to come to terms with the same material in the same serious-minded way. It's not exactly that I forgive him for the idiocy; it's more that my resistance to him can be as valuable to me as my agreement with softer, easier writers.

If we set aside all the stories in the three volumes that are about sex, and all the stories that are about men and women battling with or mocking or destroying each other—if we get rid of "The Woman Who Rode Away" and "The Princess" and "The Witch a la Mode" and so forth—we are still left with quite a few Lawrences. There is the Lawrence who was interested in the family life of the miner, and the Lawrence who was interested in rivalry or passion between men, and the Lawrence who was interested in the possession of material objects, and the Lawrence who was interested in spirits and faux spiritualism, and the Lawrence who was interested in disappointed youthful hopes and despairing middle age. Each of these Lawrences produced at least one very good story ("Odour of Chrysanthemums," "The Prussian Officer," "Things," "The Lovely Lady," and "The Shadow in the Rose Garden" are my favorites in each of these genres, respectively), and each helped to create wonderful passages even within the flawed stories.

There is sharp, unusual writing sprinkled all through the three volumes. "In town Egbert had plenty of friends, of the same ineffectual sort as himself, tampering with the arts, literature, painting, sculpture, music"—it's the word "tampering," in this sentence from "England, My England," that so brilliantly sets the quintessential Lawrence tone. "He was like a mollusc whose shell was broken"—that's the last line of "The Blind Man," and it utterly conveys the man's weak, enclosed character. Lawrence had a marvelous ear, not only for the common speech of the Midlands miner, but for the poetry of a lyrical line, the strangeness of an allegorical sentence. He knew, at times, just how far he could depart from daily speech and still keep his literary language alive. And at other times this is precisely what he *didn't* know, as if the tone-deaf Lawrence had temporarily prevailed over the perfect-pitch one.

"The Rocking-Horse Winner" is the only story, I now think, that sustains its perfect pitch from start to finish. It is also the only story whose opening lines remained preserved in my memory, ringing the bell of recognition when I read them again. (Well, this is not quite true: I also recognized the opening lines of "Odour of Chrysanthemums," but that's because Ford Madox Ford memorably reproduced them in his autobiography, to show why he fished Lawrence out of the slush pile and published him in his magazine.) There are phrases in the opening passage of "The Rocking-Horse Winner" that are purposely archaic, almost fairy-tale-like, and others that are noticeably awkward in terms of word order, and still others that are strangely vague. When Lawrence uses these strategies in other stories, the language often sounds strained or false, but here it works perfectly to set the semi-allegorical tone:

> There was a woman who was beautiful, who started with all the advantages, yet she had no luck. She married for love, and

the love turned to dust. She had bonny children, yet she felt they had been thrust upon her, and she could not love them. They looked at her coldly, as if they were finding fault with her. And hurriedly she felt she must cover up some fault in herself. Yet what it was she must cover up she never knew.

Farther down on the first page we learn of the family's financial troubles: the father's inability to hold down a lucrative job, the mother's desperation to earn some money herself. "She wracked her brains, and tried this thing and the other, but could not find anything successful." The phrase "this thing and the other" is like the unspecified widget that forms the basis of the family fortune in Henry James's *The Ambassadors*. That is, the author's very refusal to describe the particular source of income says something about his characters' feelings about sources of income in general: money is a desirable end, but the need to produce it is onerous, not to mention embarrassing. There is also a certain helplessness in the phrase, an echo of the same vague personality who wants to cover up a fault in herself without ever knowing what it is.

And for me there is a further echo as well. Reading this phrase, I recall that I read "The Rocking-Horse Winner" for the first time not in Cambridge, England, but in Palo Alto, California, when I was in high school. My mother, who was at that time a junior-college English teacher, had given her students this story to read, and she complained bitterly about one student paper which criticized "this thing and the other" as being too vague, therefore bad writing. This, my mother felt, was what incompetent English teaching had produced—firm rules about "good" writing, and therefore tone-deaf students. I had read the story recently, or read it then, and I agreed with my mother, as I do so often, still, about literary and aesthetic matters. So the little phrase "this thing and the other," though it denotes vagueness, produces in me the very opposite response: a sharp jolt of memory, a very specific carrying-back to my childhood home (a home in which, not incidentally, the mother tried this thing and the other, over the years, to bring in some supplementary income).

Lawrence himself would no doubt have understood my response, for he is the writer who said in his poem "The Piano":

> In spite of myself, the insidious mastery of song
> Betrays me back, till the heart of me weeps to belong
> To the old Sunday evenings at home . . .

This poem is, among other things, about a mother and child, as "The Rocking-Horse Winner" also is. If Lawrence was frequently bad on lovers, he was often great on sons. (And daughters. There is a wonderful scene in "Odour of Chrysanthemums" where the little girl is thrilled that her overworked, beleaguered mother has done something uncharacteristically whimsical: "'Oh, mother! . . . You've got a flower in your apron,' said the child, in a little rapture at this unusual event . . . Irritably, the mother took the flowers out from her apron-band. 'Oh, mother—don't take them out!' Annie cried, catching her hand and trying to replace the sprig.") When he is writing about sex, Lawrence seems to have no patience with children; they are a burdensome by-product, a tether to the mundane world. But when he forgets about the male-female nexus and focuses instead on the parent-child bond (which can also produce its own strange version of a male-female nexus), he is much more sympathetic. He remembers what it felt like to be a child who worries about his mother, and he can imagine what it feels like to be a mother who is invested—willingly or not—in her child.

The plot of "The Rocking-Horse Winner" is simple, and strange. The boy Paul (who is one of the few people in the story to have a name) senses that there are money worries in the family—he actually hears disembodied "voices in the house" that "simply trilled and screamed in a sort of ecstasy: 'There *must* be more money! O-h-h, there *must* be more money! Oh, now, now-w!'" So Paul comes up with a solution. He rides his rocking-horse intently, furiously, until he "gets there," and at that point he knows with supernatural certainty the name of the winner of an upcoming horse race. Abetted by the family gardener and eventually by his turf-loving uncle, Paul places increasingly large sums of money on the horses, and he repeatedly wins. He is thrilled to be "lucky" (his mother has told him that the family is "unlucky" about money, which is the only kind of luck she cares about), but he is also driven, because however much he raises in this strange manner, the house always clamors for more. In the end, Paul dies from the intensity of his effort (some unspecified brain fever, clearly linked to his desperate rocking, is what actually kills him), but not before he comes up with the name of the Derby winner and earns a fortune for his mother. The last lines of the story are spoken by the uncle to the mother: "'My God, Hester, you're eighty-odd thousand to the good, and a poor devil of a son to the bad. But, poor devil, poor devil, he's best gone out of a life where he rides his rocking-horse to find a winner!'"

There is no moral, as such, to this story—or rather, any moral we may be tempted to draw from it is totally inadequate and ridiculous. Don't value money too much? Uselessly platitudinous. Don't let your children get wind of your financial worries? Impossible to fulfill. Don't take supernatural advice when betting on horses? You see the problem. The story is in every way bigger than any point it may have. It creates a feeling, but even the feeling is ambiguous: a mixture of horror, and excitement, and pity, and despairing wonder. (Despairing wonder, it seems to me, is the prevailing tone of the uncle's last lines.) And it does so against the most tremendous odds. Any warnings about gambling are bound to seem two-edged, coming from an author who bets that we will fall for a story like this. But we do.

When I was younger, I simply accepted the story as a success. Now, I can't help marveling that it does succeed, and wondering how Lawrence managed to pull it off. It uses the same elements that sink many of the other stories—spiritualism, dominating mother, sudden death, sexually charged imagery, exclamatory excess—and yet rather than giving in to them, it molds them to its own purposes. Like the Lawrence stories of my memory, and unlike most of the stories I reread this time, "The Rocking-Horse Winner" is a model of restraint and delicate craftsmanship. There are no mistaken sentences; every line, every word does its job and then some. But this is accomplished without any sense of undue authorial control. On the contrary, the story feels as free as an anonymous folktale, as loose as a song. Its progress seems inevitable in the way that only the most impersonal literature does. And yet it has Lawrence's thumbprint all over it, in the sense that only he, of all the writers I know, could have written this story.

You can pick at the texture of the tale and find some of the threads that give it its richness. There is the way it reveals and withholds names, for instance. We hear a lot of racehorses' names (Daffodil, Sansovino, Singhalese, Lively Spark, Malabar: all the winners, and a few others besides), but the rocking-horse itself has no name. The uncle and the gardener have names, but the sisters, the father, and the mother do not—until the last line, when the mother turns out to be Hester. Lawrence, as we know from his remarkable *Studies in Classic American Literature*, was fascinated by Hester Prynne, the heroine of *The Scarlet Letter*, and she too was notoriously a mother. Paul is, of course, the biblical apostle, as well as the hero of Lawrence's own *Sons and Lovers*, the autobiographical Paul Morel. But it doesn't do to make too much of these allusions. The story would not lose one bit of its power if we had never heard of Hester or Paul. For the power of the names in "The Rocking-Horse Winner" is largely incantatory. Like the notes of the "great black piano appassionato" in Lawrence's poem, they exercise "the insidious mastery of song," calling to us even as (though surely not in the same way) they call to the boy on his rocking-horse.

And if the names are lyrical, they are also novelistic, literary. Conjuring specific individuals out of nothingness and giving them evocative names has been the great privilege of the fiction writer, from Cervantes on down. To believe too faithfully in the made-up names has always been a sign of madness. Yet it remains a temptation. That we can be too old for this sort of game ("'Surely you're too big for a rocking-horse!' his mother had remonstrated") and yet still want to ride into the imaginative terrain of childhood and memory and belief: this is a truth that is repeatedly forced on the writer of a book about rereading.

The huge Lawrence I once loved has boiled down, for me, into this single story. No matter; I can still cherish him in this reduced, pocket-sized form. What makes Lawrence a special case is that time has not helped me to understand him. Reading and rereading "The Rocking-Horse Winner" only makes it seem more mysterious, more complicated, more logically incomprehensible. It looks so simple—its very texture is the texture of folktale or ghost-story simplicity—and yet it refuses to yield up its secrets. I imagine it will work on me forever, like a card trick that is not, in fact, a trick, but a mathematically complicated display of numerical properties. I will never really figure out how it works. Lawrence himself felt about any piece of literature that "once it is fathomed, once it is known and its meaning is fixed or established, it is dead." He would, I hope, have been pleased to learn that "The Rocking-Horse Winner" is among the works that remain persistently alive for me.

THE FACE BEHIND
THE PAGE

~~~

Probably no writer has
been more important to me, as a direct and traceable influence, than George Orwell. I have spent nearly thirty years trying to sound like him in my own essays, and I have spent over twenty years looking for other people who sounded like him so I could print their essays in my magazine. One of my alternate names for *The Threepenny Review*, when I was developing the idea for it in late 1979, was *Wigan Pier*; and though Brecht ultimately won out on the title, it was Orwell who seemed to me to embody the spirit of the enterprise. For years, whenever I found a good, new writer, especially one capable of writing eloquently on political subjects like homelessness or the death penalty, I would think of him or her as a new George Orwell, and to some extent I still think this way.

But after recently rereading Orwell's essays—among which I count his three book-length essays, *Down and Out in Paris and London, The Road to Wigan Pier,* and *Homage to Catalonia*—I have come to realize that the Orwell I carried around in my mind all these years is not quite the one on the page. They are not unrelated; I can still see the man I once hero-worshipped glimmering behind certain glorious paragraphs of English prose. But I can also see other things that are less appealing, including Orwell's occasional tendency to pontificate, his unwarranted faith in his own eccentric convictions, his reliance on false logic, and his sometimes incapacitating degree of emotional blindness. These qualities, too, have probably influenced my style, in ways that I am still struggling to escape, and the struggle is itself part of the current tension in my relationship to Orwell.

I am hardly a singular case, in this respect. Orwell was, it seems, put on this earth to elicit or exacerbate tense relationships. Starting during his lifetime, but particularly since his death in 1950, he has won the fervid allegiance of a huge number of readers and writers, many of whom hate one another's opinions and approaches. He has been taken into a lot of different camps and elected totemic leader in all of them, with the result that people are always squabbling over who really owns George Orwell. I used to think this was because other readers couldn't really see him for what he was. That is, *they* were all wrong about him (those right-wingers who championed him as an anti-Communist, those schoolteachers who employed him to teach "transparent" style), and only I was right. It was very Orwellian of me to think this. The adjective has come to suggest institutionalized duplicity and totalitarianism because of its now-inevitable connection with *1984*, but I mean it in a different sense: it was very like Orwell, in his own writing. And of course the two meanings are connected. It is no accident that Orwell was able to invent the concept of doublethink, because he practiced it so well himself—not just in the way that all good writers do, as a form of rich, multifarious, ongoing self-contradiction, but in a very specific way that involved blocking out, or forgetting, the parts of reality and of himself that conflicted with what he wanted to say at a given moment. Orwell's own special version of doublethink lay in the simultaneous use and denial of self-contradiction. It is this quality which so effectively ties all his critics in knots.

And the reason it confounds us is that we are drawn to Orwell—or at least we imagine we are drawn to him—by his singular clarity. You can call it by other names: straightforwardness, sincerity, honesty, directness. I have called it by all those names myself, and I fully believed what I was saying at the time. So when later I came to hear the underlying contradictions in his essays, I felt momentarily betrayed. (I have an embarrassed memory, for instance, of ranting, in front of an introductory literature class I was team-teaching in 1977 or so, about what a liar George Orwell was—even though I myself had admiringly put him on the reading list. When the class hour was over, my fellow teacher, acting on behalf of the understandably confused students, asked me to please refrain in future from last-minute changes of heart.) And then, in truly Orwellian fashion, I would forget my sense of betrayal and go back to the hero-worship mode. One or the other: it was as if I couldn't hold the two positions in my mind at once. I had, it seemed, absorbed my idol's methods all too well.

Let us pause here to examine the trail of documentary evidence. For once, I can offer you something other than my own memories; for once, there is tangible proof of what I thought during a long-ago reading. At this very moment, I hold in my hands a thirty-six-page essay (thirty-eight, if you count the bibliography) that I submitted to Cambridge University in partial fulfillment of the English Tripos, Part Two. It was, in other words, my little dissertation, my miniature thesis. The essay is entitled "Why I Believe George Orwell: A Study of His Rhetoric," and its cover sheet bears the date "20 March, 1975"—my twenty-third birthday, a submission date

I undoubtedly saw as cementing the connection between my subject and myself.

Reading this essay is for me now an excruciating experience. It is not that the ideas and arguments are uniformly terrible. Sometimes they even verge on being good. But on page after page, I see that I have hit the nail glancingly—never on the head, but always right on the very edge, so that my blow twists the point uselessly while failing to drive it home. I am so wedded to the idea that Orwell is honest, or truthful, or sincere (and I use all these terms in loose, baggy, logic-defying ways) that I cannot even begin to understand the limitations he has imposed on himself. To make matters worse, I have taken on those very limitations in my own style—but completely unconsciously, and therefore ineffectually. I will offer, as a compromise between your delectation and my humiliation, but a single example. "When one says of a man, 'He is telling the truth,' one may mean either that he is being as honest as possible and refraining from intentional lies, or that he is stating some fact which corresponds to an objective reality," I say in my best pseudo-British, faux logical mode. "The two are not necessarily synonymous. A man may tell the truth as he sees it and still be wrong in an objective sense. When I refer to Orwell in this essay as someone who appears to tell the truth, I am speaking only of the first kind of truth, the kind that has to do with honesty and sincerity. I have no way of verifying the objective truth of most of his factual statements, and even if I did that would not concern me here." *And why the hell not?* I want to snarl down the corridor of twenty-five years. My essay sounds like a feeble imitation of Orwell's manly English straightforwardness, but with all the dark underlying complexity taken out. And that's partly because I failed to hear those complications in *his* writing—willfully failed, despite all sorts of opportunities for confrontation. The whole essay, it seems to me now, is just a series of missed opportunities.

Attached with a paper clip to my surviving copy of the essay is a yellow sheet of unlined paper, closely written on both sides in the inimitably inscrutable handwriting of Christopher Ricks. I suppose everyone has a teacher who, more than anyone else, has shaped her or his intellectual life. In my case it is Christopher, who has been there in the background of my writing and thinking since I was nineteen years old. In many ways we are not at all alike, but that, on the whole, has been a useful thing—I have not been tempted to confuse myself with him, as I so mistakenly did with George Orwell. Still, different as we are, we have come to hold very similar opinions about my Orwell essay, as I now learn by reexamining this note from October of 1976. (Here, at any rate, is a rereading that represents a change. In 1976, I am sure, I simply met Christopher's careful critique with a wounded, he-doesn't-like-it reaction. Taking criticism —*understanding* criticism—was never my strong point, especially at that age.)

On this always yellow but now yellowing page, Christopher astutely takes apart my simplistic distinction between objective and subjective truth. He also makes exactly the same criticism I would now make about my handling of the word "honest." With his usual take-no-prisoners accuracy, he points out to me the way "you not only *limit* but *debilitate* yr. own enquiry by so much circumscribing it, so that the end is curiously academic and cloistered. The 'techniques' (as, in my judgment, you so misleadingly or tendentiously call them) get so divorced from serious moral/intellectual enquiry as to be no more than a bag of tricks." He means, as I meant, Orwell's techniques, but the statement applies so well to my own "bag of tricks" (not to mention most academic literary criticism written between that day and this) that it serves, from this distance, as a persistently valuable admonishment. Even more pertinent, at this particular juncture, is Christopher's observation that "you seem to me to avert yr. eyes from things wh. you yourself notice." Yes. Exactly. It is, I'm afraid, a bad habit of mine in general—but it is also something I learned, in this case, specifically from George Orwell.

As a literary critic (which he frequently was, though he would never have called himself that), Orwell had a handful of incomparable strengths and some equally salient weaknesses. Even the best of the literary essays—and here I'm thinking of pieces like "Inside the Whale," "Politics vs. Literature," and the true gem of the batch, "Charles Dickens"— are infused with both. When Orwell is good, it is because he has spotted something strange or unusual in what an author is doing and has allowed himself to pay close attention to it. When he is bad, it is because he is averting his eyes from the very oddities that have captured his attention, generally in order to make the literary work fit into some preconceived theory he has about what literature is, or should be. We aren't used to thinking of Orwell as a theorist because his style is so relentlessly empirical, emphasizing concreteness over abstraction, Anglo-Saxon brevity over Latinate floridity, colloquialism over formality, and so forth. But he often *is* a theorist, and usually quite a bad one. "Politics and the English Language," for instance, is almost all theory, and for me it is among the least successful of his essays: the points are banal where true, the examples are frequently dated or inaccurate, and the exhorting, instructive voice falls dead on the page.

But even in his good essays Orwell is constantly struggling with his own tendency toward exhortation. He understands that literature—especially the literature he cares most deeply about—is not identical with propaganda, but he invariably wants to drag it back in that direction. In "Inside the Whale" we find him insisting that "at bottom it is always a writer's tendency, his 'purpose,' his 'message,' that makes him liked or disliked." That essay was first published in 1940; by 1946, in "Politics vs. Literature," his essay about Jonathan Swift, he has reached a slightly more complicated position. Acknowledging that a book need not be politically progressive or even true to be good, Orwell suggests that

> the best books of any age have always been written from several different viewpoints, some of them palpably more false than others. In so far as a writer is a propagandist, the most one can ask of him is that he shall genuinely believe in what he is saying, and that it shall not be something blazingly silly . . . The views that a writer holds must be compatible with sanity, in the medical sense, and with the power of continuous thought: beyond that what we ask of him is talent, which is probably another name for conviction.

Even here, though, he is obsessively focused on a writer's "views," which is simply a slightly more expansive way of referring to "purpose" or "message." (I'm leaving aside the touchy issue of how we are actually to determine when those views are "palpably" more false or "blazingly" silly; such adverbs represent Orwell at his least helpful.) When he does, for a moment, try to consider the other levels at which a book like *Gulliver's Travels* operates on us, he comes up with something feeble like "It is true that the literary quality of a book is to some small extent separable from its subject-matter. Some people have a native gift for using words, as some people have a naturally 'good eye' at games. It is largely a question of timing and of instinctively knowing how much emphasis to use." Phrases such as "native gift" and "instinctively" are gesturing toward a new and potentially fruitful line of argument, but Orwell doesn't want to go there.

This insistence on "views" and "convictions" and "purpose" means that Orwell has, finally, a very narrow view of authorial intention. (Just as I did, apparently, in writing about Orwell: "being as honest as possible and refraining from *intentional* lies.") As a result, most of what we actually derive from a novel—that is, the stuff of life, the felt and perceived texture of reality, shaped for our benefit by an intervening sensibility—falls, for Orwell, into some kind of no-man's-land that doesn't really count. He's capable of seeing all the many-sided and contradictory ways in which a novel is working on him, but he doesn't want to give the author credit for them. So, for instance, in his Dickens essay, he observes:

> Psychologically the latter part of *Great Expectations* is about the best thing Dickens ever did; throughout this part of the book one feels, "Yes, that is just how Pip would have behaved." But the point is that in the matter of Magwitch, Dickens identifies with Pip, and his attitude is at bottom snobbish. The result is that Magwitch belongs to the same queer class of characters as Falstaff and, probably, Don Quixote—characters who are more pathetic than the author intended.

Talk about averting your eyes. How could pathos and sympathy ever be more effectively employed than they were by Cervantes and Shakespeare? And even Dickens is more in command of the situation than Orwell acknowledges—or rather, his authorial self-contradictoriness is used far more skillfully than Orwell is willing to credit. But it is precisely this kind of doubleness, in which unconscious effects work side by side with conscious ones, that Orwell is worst at perceiving. And that blindness to the essential byways of a literary work leads him into occasional idiotic pronouncements, such as his remark about *King Lear:* "One wicked daughter would have been quite enough, and Edgar is a superfluous character: indeed it would probably be a better play if Gloucester and both his sons were eliminated." It is this kind of thing that gives frank singlemindedness a bad name.

Orwell is of course not as singleminded as he believes himself to be—or perhaps I should say, as he wishes himself to be. He seems to think, at times, that subtlety and complication are somewhat despicable middle-class qualities, the sort of thing we should be willing to dispense with if we are to march forward into a socialist future. At other times—particularly in *The Road to Wigan Pier*, which now strikes me as his best and most coherent book—he has more mixed and affectionate feelings about the things that go with being middle class. What he has to say about himself, in that book, sheds a great deal of light on his critique of Charles Dickens, especially in regard to the accusation of snobbishness. "All my notions—notions of good and evil, of pleasant and unpleasant, of funny and serious, of ugly and beautiful—are essentially *middle-class* notions," he confesses in *The Road to Wigan Pier*:

> My taste in books and food and clothes, my sense of humor, my table manners, my turns of speech, my accent, even the characteristic movements of my body, are the products of a special kind of upbringing and a special niche about half-way up the social hierarchy. When I grasp this I grasp that it is no use clapping a proletarian on the back and telling him that he is as good a man as I am; if I want real contact with him, I have got to make an effort for which very likely I am unprepared. For to get outside the class-racket I have got to suppress not merely my private snobbishness, but most of my other tastes and prejudices as well. I have got to alter myself so completely that at the end I should hardly be recognizable as the same person.

Being "recognizable as the same person" is a crucial value for Orwell, though what he means by it can be a little difficult to pin down. As he tells us at the end of the Dickens essay, when he reads "any strongly individual piece of writing" he can see "a face somewhere behind the page"—"not necessarily the actual face of the writer" but "the face that the writer *ought* to have." Orwell's ringing description of

Dickens's imagined face, "the face of a man who is always fighting against something, but who fights in the open and is not frightened, the face of a man who is *generously angry*—in other words, of a nineteenth-century liberal, a free intelligence, a type hated with equal hatred by all the smelly little orthodoxies which are now contending for our souls," has often been taken as a self-portrait. (I took it as one myself in the concluding sentence of my 1975 essay.) Yet the important thing to remember here is that Orwell cannot be seen as *consciously* applying this description to himself; if he were, it would seem uncharacteristically and self-defeatingly immodest. For the analogy to work, we must feel we are drawing the comparison ourselves. Orwell's skill as an essayist leads us almost inevitably to this conclusion, but surely we would hesitate to call this the "intention" or "purpose" or "message" of the essay. Rather, it is one of those semi-unconscious, deeply intuitive, utterly polished maneuvers for which I would want to give the author full credit, even if Orwell himself would refuse to do so.

I use the term "utterly polished" with some confidence, because I see now that Orwell didn't start out this way, however good his instincts may have been. This insight has not come to me easily. The old Wendy—or rather, the young Wendy, the author of "Why I Believe George Orwell"—did not distinguish different phases of her hero's development. She wanted him to have emerged full-blown from Zeus's head, his quiver already filled with choice rhetorical arrows. (It's strange, that word "rhetoric" in my subtitle. At that point it was linked in my mind with artificiality, manipulation, inauthenticity, so in defending Orwell's truthtelling at the same time as I was acknowledging his use of rhetoric, I was trying to persuade myself that the inauthentic could be used in an authentic way. I apparently succeeded, for I now employ the word "rhetoric," in the privacy of my own editorial mind, whenever I am trying to think about my own or another writer's relationship to the presumed reader. The word has completely lost its negative connotation for me — or perhaps it would be more accurate to say that I have given up on the idea of a naive authenticity.)

Before I returned to George Orwell this time, I would have said that the voice of *Down and Out in Paris and London* was essentially the same as the voice of *The Road to Wigan Pier*. Reading them one after the other, just now, I was shocked to discover the extent to which this isn't true. In the four years that separated the publication of the two books, Orwell became Orwell. Politically, he was to be changed by the events chronicled in *Homage to Catalonia*, but as a voice speaking to us in reasonable, slightly humorous, often very personal tones, he was all there by late 1936 or early 1937. In *Down and Out* Orwell presented himself almost as an Isherwoodian camera, a mere instrument through which the sights and sounds of urban distress could be transmitted to us. By the time he wrote *The Road to Wigan Pier*, he had learned to put himself into the picture.

The man behind *Down and Out* is pretty much a cipher: all we know is that he is young and English, he is tall but not very strong, he has a moustache which he has to shave off at one point, and he is squeamish about dirt and bugs. (This last was to become one of the running themes of Orwell's writing, up to and including the late, great essay "Such, Such Were the Joys," which goes into thrilling, excruciating detail about the filth he encountered in his prep school. Even the heavily political *Homage to Catalonia* begins its account of war by focusing on dirt, smells, and excrement, though there Orwell seems to deny his own predilection by observing, "Dirt is a thing people make too much fuss about." Well, maybe — but if so, then he is one of those people.) What we glean of Orwell, in *Down and Out*, we glean on our own; he is not going to offer us anything directly. But by *The Road to Wigan Pier* he has decided to tell us things. He still doesn't tell us everything (even "Such, Such Were the Joys" doesn't do that—the withholding of information in a spirit of seeming confidentiality is one of Orwell's greatest abilities), but he does tell us enough to make us feel we know him personally.

One of the things he decides to tell us about is class—not just the class of the unemployed miners he is living among, and not just the class of the sneering conservatives who think those miners are loafers, but his own class. "I was born into the lower-upper-middle class," he says in *The Road to Wigan Pier*, and he links this observation to his childhood fear of tramps and laborers, his squeamishness about dirt and smells, his ingrained snobbishness about people who slurp their tea. And this in turn makes him better able to mock the sort of pose he took when he wrote *Down and Out in Paris and London*, the willfully class-ignoring stance which he characterizes in *Wigan Pier* as "Let's pal up and get our shoulders to the wheel and remember that we're all equal, and what the devil does it matter if I know what kind of ties to wear and you don't, and I drink my soup comparatively quietly and you drink yours with the noise of water going down a waste-pipe." (It takes someone who has actually *felt* this way to put in the detail about the waste-pipe noise.) In *Down and Out*, he allowed us to believe that this period of brutal poverty had simply fallen upon him, so that he had no alternative to dishwashing and tramping; in *The Road to Wigan Pier*, he looks back over that time and describes it as a purposeful scourging of his middle-class self, something he did to alleviate his own guilt.

I warm to the Orwell of *The Road to Wigan Pier*, despite or perhaps even because of his occasional tendency to break into a rant against health-food faddists, free-love advocates, bearded sandal-wearers, and all the other types roundly if somewhat inexplicably hated by the Lucky Jims of the world. In contrast, the narrator of *Down and Out in Paris and*

London is a rather cold fish. Reporting on the casual brutalities of life among the Parisian poor, he could almost be Jean Genet or Paul Bowles or William Burroughs. (Or, for that matter, Salvador Dali—which would explain the special, insightful animus behind "Benefit of Clergy.") He aims to shock us with his tales of squalor and abuse, but he himself remains deadpan: "He was a curious specimen," for instance, is all he has to say about Charlie, whose grotesque tale of sexual cruelty he renders from Charlie's point of view.

Perhaps more tellingly, the "I" we meet in *Down and Out* is a frequent, self-admitted liar. He lies to his landlady about the rent, to his employers about his intentions, to fellow travelers about the sights of London, and to officials in the tramp compounds about his name and profession. He lies for the fun of it and he also lies, sometimes, to deceive himself. "The mass of the rich and the poor are differentiated by their incomes and nothing else, and the average millionaire is only the average dishwasher in a new suit . . . Everyone who has mixed on equal terms with the poor knows this quite well," he says, sounding like a parody of the unthinking "let's pal up" democrat Orwell mocks in *The Road to Wigan Pier*. Above all, he lies to us about his politics, repeatedly pretending that he has none. This was evidently the result of a conscious rhetorical decision—Orwell must have felt that his report on poverty would seem more believable if it came from someone without a political ax to grind—but it contradicts everything he wrote before and after *Down and Out*. Even as Eric Blair, in the 1931 essay "The Hanging," he had displayed strong political opinions about capital punishment and imperial justice. So the effect, for those of us who know the rest of Orwell, is to make *Down and Out in Paris and London* seem close to fiction—and indeed my Penguin copy of it, purchased in England in 1974, is actually labeled "Fiction/Literature," whereas my *Road to Wigan Pier*, bought at the same time, is classified as "Autobiography." It is interesting to imagine the kind of fiction writer Orwell might have become if he had taken his *Down and Out* mode further in the same direction. Not a very good one, I think. He lacked the chilly detachment of a Bowles, the desire for abasement of a Burroughs, the attention-getting need of a Genet. His capacity to represent the lower depths was always, in this respect, limited.

But *Down and Out in Paris and London* does contain, in embryonic form, the trait which was to make Orwell the writer he was. "I find that anything outrageously strange generally ends by fascinating me even when I abominate it," he says of himself, accurately, in *The Road to Wigan Pier*. It is this ability to see the outrageously strange from the standpoint of firm reasonableness—to recognize its strangeness and to voice the outrage—that underlies all his best essays. Sometimes we share the outrage and sometimes we can't quite understand what's causing it, but either way it is useful to us, because it helps us see things we otherwise might not have noticed.

And this, in turn, is linked to the quality in Orwell's writing that now gives me the greatest pleasure: his reliance on the seemingly irrelevant but actually quite important detail. In typical fashion, he perceived this strategy in another writer without remarking it in himself—and, equally characteristically, he saw only half the story: "The outstanding, unmistakable mark of Dickens's writing is the *unnecessary detail*." Among the examples he gave from Dickens's work, the one I remembered best over the years was the one about the machinery in *Hard Times* that went "monotonously up and down, like the head of an elephant in a state of melancholy madness." (Actually, this was a slightly false memory—that is, Orwell did cite that line from Dickens, but as an "impressionistic touch" rather than an "unnecessary detail"; he gives two *other* examples of unnecessary details.) Perhaps I recalled that elephant because it joined up in my mind with

Orwell's own elephant, the one he felt obliged to shoot, which was "beating his bunch of grass against his knees, with that preoccupied grandmotherly air that elephants have." Irrelevant as this detail may have been to the procedures governing policemen in Burma, it is certainly not *unnecessary* in the essay "Shooting an Elephant," as anyone who thinks about the phrase "shooting a grandmother" can see.

In classifying Dickens's literary flourishes as inessential, Orwell was ignoring the strongest element in his own style: its capacity to make us discover the truth analogically. Time and again, he offers us a seemingly irrelevant observation that turns out, if you look at it closely enough, to be central to his argument. In *The Road to Wigan Pier*, for instance, he comments on the "row upon row of little red houses, all much liker than two peas (where did that expression come from? Peas have great individuality)." The parenthetical remark may seem a throwaway bit of humor, until you stop to consider that it comes in a book about specific conditions and manners among the people who tend to get lumped indifferentiably together as the "masses."

When I was twenty-three, I took Orwell too much at face value. I read him too literally, and so I missed a vast amount of what he was offering me. When he called such details unnecessary or irrelevant, I believed him. One of his own "irrelevant" details that I seized on at the time—that I noticed and, somehow, failed to notice—was his habit of bringing up how old he was when he first read a book. I captured two examples: "I must have been about nine years old when I first read *David Copperfield*" and, about *Gulliver's Travels*, "I read it first when I was eight—one day short of eight, to be exact, for I stole and furtively read the copy which was to be given me next day on my eighth birthday." And then, with a degree of pomposity that only the young can summon up, I followed this delicious quote with the comment, "Now, there is no way in which Orwell's eighth birthday can have any logical bearing on the merits of Swift." Don't you just want to *smack* her? And do you find it as incredible as I do that this young person should have grown into a woman who now feels obliged to tell you what *she* was reading at the age of eight, or eleven, or nineteen? My only excuse for her is that over the years, slowly, secretly, and unwittingly, she may have been learning something from George Orwell even as she was failing to understand him.

LATE SHAKESPEARE

Wʜᴇɴ ɪ ᴡᴀѕ ʏᴏᴜɴɢᴇʀ I
didn't think much of the strange romances that Shakespeare
wrote toward the end of his life—or, to put it more accurately, I didn't think much about them. I am sure I read both
The Winter's Tale and *The Tempest* when I was in my twenties.
I read just about every Shakespeare play then (with the possible exception of the dubious *King John*), because I took at
least four Shakespeare seminars during my graduate school
years at Berkeley. The department was very strong in Shakespeare in those days—this was the late 1970s—and since
my Cambridge education had helped me test out of the
other required areas, Shakespeare seemed the obvious thing
to do.

Like most people of that age, I was drawn to the
tragedies. *Antony and Cleopatra* was my favorite for a long
time, and I still think it is one of Shakespeare's greatest plays
—I reread it recently with all the old pleasure and illumina-
tion. But that was the problem, in a way: I had been so famil-

iar with this play in my youth, known its singularly expressive passages so well, that when I came back to it again it was a bit like reading the Hopkins and Dickinson poems I had memorized as a child. The lines were engraved in my memory, etched too deep for change. I had had my *Antony and Cleopatra* experience and was not, apparently, going to have another, different one.

In those days I also cared a great deal about *Othello, King Lear, Macbeth,* and, less consistently, *Hamlet.* I have seen each of these plays performed many times, partly because I sought them out, but also because they were among the Shakespeare plays repeatedly being produced on various stages in Britain and America. And there were other plays that reappeared unbidden: in the last thirty years, for example, I have attended no fewer than three productions — all, in their own ways, quite memorable — of the relatively obscure *Richard II.* So it seems odd to me that I have never seen a live performance of either *The Tempest* or *The Winter's Tale.* Reading them now, I want desperately to see them onstage — not because they are more incomplete as literary artifacts than the tragedies (whatever that would mean, about a play), but because they cry out for the psychological and emotional amplification that only great actors can introduce. Perhaps the tragedies cry out for it too, but since I have seen both good and bad productions of *Lear,* and *Hamlet,* and *Othello,* I know exactly what actors can do with them, or to them. With *The Tempest* and *The Winter's Tale,* I must still rely on my imagination, my guesswork.

My guesswork has become a bit more inspired over the years, mainly because I know more about actors now than I did when I was young. In the mid-1990s, when I was in my early forties, I wrote a book about an English stage director, and that got me intensely involved in the world of the theater for a few years. I know, for instance, that actors are a superstitious lot — they really do say "the Scottish play" when they mean *Macbeth*—so I can understand some of the terrible power they might attribute to *The Tempest*. Only an actor who felt immune to the conjuring forces, or who truly believed himself to be at the end of his career, could comfortably deliver Prospero's renunciatory lines, from "this rough magic / I abjure" through the closing soliloquy that begins "Now my charms are all o'erthrown." It's not just that Prospero is toying with god-given powers or swearing oaths, though these are certainly things that would make actors nervous. (I imagine that's partly what makes them nervous about *Macbeth*. Actors have been aware of the curious power of "performative utterances" since long before either J. L. Austin or Judith Butler got hold of the notion.) The scarier thing, for an actor, is that Prospero is so clearly speaking to us as a man of the theater: a designer who stages tempests, a director/playwright who manipulates the other actors, and, especially in the epilogue, an actor himself—a man who stands alone onstage addressing us directly as an audience, locating himself in some indeterminable place between the imaginary character and the fellow human being.

But the word "between" is wrong. Prospero's final speech presumes—as do all great theatrical epilogues—that the man and the character have become merged in the actor, at least for the duration of this performance, so that even the closest witnesses (we, the audience) will not be able to tell one from the other. The importance of this moment helps determine, I think, which actors will make great Prosperos. The actor not only needs to be very powerful and persuasive; he also needs to be a man of the theater, not just a movie star imported for this one occasion. And it's best if he is old enough to have a vast theatrical career behind him—preferably a career that sticks in our memories, so that we at some level recall him in all those other roles as he is bidding adieu to this particular one.

Prospero's epilogue is thrilling because it does two seemingly opposite things at once. It builds on our sense that we know this character intimately, and yet it also suggests that he is not the same powerful magician we have spent the past two or three hours with. *That* Prospero did not need our help; *that* Prospero did not even acknowledge our existence. Now he claims to be utterly dependent on us. Yet even in denying his own magical powers, the actor is using them:

> Now my charms are all o'erthrown,
> And what strength I have's mine own,
> Which is most faint. Now 'tis true
> I must be here confined by you,
> Or sent to Naples. Let me not,
> Since I have my dukedom got
> And pardoned the deceiver, dwell
> In this bare island by your spell;
> But release me from my bands
> With the help of your good hands.
> Gentle breath of yours my sails
> Must fill, or else my project fails,
> Which was to please. Now I want
> Spirits to enforce, art to enchant;
> And my ending is despair
> Unless I be relieved by prayer,
> Which pierces so that it assaults
> Mercy itself and frees all faults.
> As you from crimes would pardoned be,
> Let your indulgence set me free.

These lines are both within and outside the play, spoken at once by Prospero, the actor playing Prospero, and the playwright himself. And this slight blurring, this barely perceptible but absolutely essential indeterminability, is what gives certain words so much latitude. Whose strength is "mine"? And where is "here"? Is it really *our* spell that keeps Prospero onstage—that is, do we really have the power to "release" him, or does he instead "pardon" us? (And what "crimes" have we committed, anyway? Might they include, as Prospero's do, the crime of deriving pleasure from the confusion of others?) Whose, exactly, is "my project . . . Which was to please"? This, it seems to me, is where we most clearly hear Shakespeare's own voice. For while the actor can be immediately rewarded by the applause of "your good hands," it is the playwright who will benefit from the praise of our "gentle breath," those word-of-mouth recommendations and positive reviews that will bring other audiences to the theater. And when that happens, the "you" of this speech will be entirely changed as well. We are in this position of power on just this one occasion, because we happen to be at this one performance. It is a performance that, according to the epilogue, cannot end until we bring it to a close. In other words, our only power is the power to dissolve, with our clapping, the very circumstances that give us power. Prospero, in this final speech, asks us to become like Prospero—to exercise our power and thereby relinquish it. Only if we do so can he cease being Prospero.

If I had analyzed this speech as a graduate student, I would no doubt have been able to locate all the doubleness and tripleness, all the theatrical allusiveness. But I would not necessarily have been able to understand the feeling such a speech can create. I have, in the years since then, become a connoisseur of epilogues; they are often, for me, the moment in which the magic of the theater is at its most powerful, just before it disintegrates. I love to be invited in elegant rhyme to applaud—or rather, I love the fact that my conventional applause has been built into the very texture of the play, so that in bowing to the convention I am simultaneously expressing my affection for the performance and becoming a part of it myself. And just as my years of closely watching the theater have made me more attuned to scene changes and intermissions and entrances and exits—all

those things which are supposedly outside the play itself—
they have also made me focus more than ever on this moment at which the play ceases, for the night, to exist. It is a
vanishing act that, when properly done, never fails to move
and amaze me.

The Tempest, more than any other Shakespeare play, is
about this miraculous joint venture that comes into being for
the duration—for the two or three or four hours that we, the
actors and the audience, spend together—and then disappears. It is a play in which (as Jan Kott and others have
pointed out) stage time pretty much equals real time: the action takes place over an elapsed period of four hours, just as
an afternoon performance at the Globe, complete with a long
intermission, might have done. It begins with a tempest that
turns out not to be a real tempest (as if it were one of those
Brian DePalma films with a fake "cinematic" beginning),
and in doing so asks us to consider the extent to which *any*
tempest, in a play, could be considered a real tempest. In
fact, it is by calling attention to its own theatricality so frequently and so successfully—by making us think about de-
ception, and belief, and manipulativeness, and transformation, and the staginess of musical accompaniment—that *The
Tempest* comes to seem so much a part of our own felt reality.
As a play about being at a play, it must surely be one of the
most realistic dramas ever written: we are indeed witnessing
a contrived performance, as we ourselves can verify, so Prospero's statements to that effect all carry an extra measure of
truth.

It is, of course, a play about many other things as well—
no, not "as well," because that suggests the meanings sit side
by side, whereas what they really do is follow from one another, spring from within each other. For instance, the play is
clearly about power: among other things, about the power of
the Prosperos of the world over the Calibans of the world,
and about the understandable but inconvenient desire of the

Calibans to resist. In Shakespeare's own time, Caliban might well have been equated with the newly conquered American Indians. (There is strong internal evidence that Shakespeare was familiar with both Montaigne's 1603 essay "Of the Cannibals" and the Council of Virginia's description of the settling of the Virginia colony in 1609.) In the nineteenth century, and particularly after the Sepoy Mutiny, an English audience might have been led to think about the British East India Company's role on the subcontinent. If performed in Belfast or Dublin in the late twentieth century, *The Tempest* would undoubtedly have reminded its spectators of "the Troubles." This year, if it were put on in Jerusalem, it would seem to refer to Israel and the Palestinians. These meanings are not exactly in the play, but nor are they totally outside it. Since Shakespeare wrote *The Tempest*, there has never been a period when somebody was not depriving somebody else of his native land; this is not an aspect of the play that is ever, alas, likely to become dated or meaningless.

But our feelings about power in *The Tempest* do not come to us with the starkness of international news headlines. We react in very complicated, personal ways to both Prospero and Caliban. I found Prospero, on this reading, much less sympathetic than I had remembered him, and Caliban much more so. But I was also aware of how much good actors could do in both roles to bring my responses back toward the middle ground—Prospero by being irresistibly charismatic, Caliban by being actively repellent. And we would be conscious, in a stage performance, of how effectively those actors' powers were being used on us. So that too would give us an insight into this concept of "power." It would cease to be an abstraction and become something we could feel: the play's ideas about power, that is, would spring at us out of its ideas about theatrical manipulation.

It is easy to see the appeal of Caliban. That pomposity-puncturing, earthy, irritable character—that Sancho Panza, if you will—is always fun to like. What surprises me more is my distrust, even distaste, for Prospero. He is, after all, the hero of the play, possibly its only real character, and most of the beautiful, memorable speeches belong to him. But he is also a terrible windbag (Miranda is in danger of falling asleep during his first long exposition) and an unquestioning believer in his own rightness. Don Quixote too had these flaws, so why do I love the crazy Spanish knight and faintly dislike, at times, the Shakespearean magician? Perhaps because the Don *is* crazy: his foolishness, like that of Dostoyevsky's idiot, makes him infinitely more bearable. If Prospero is crazy, it is in a completely insulated way. And the play shares his solipsism, even stems from it, so that there is no ground outside of Prospero's terrain for us to stand on. If we are not on his island, we are totally at sea and in danger of drowning.

I do not mean to suggest that Prospero's mixed character is a flaw in the play; on the contrary, it is one of its uniquely Shakespearean virtues. Getting us to identify with distinctly problematic, self-engrossed, larger-than-life characters is one of Shakespeare's specialties. And in this case—perhaps in this case alone—he causes us to feel this ambivalent affection for a character who is not ultimately brought low by external circumstances. Cleopatra must lose Antony and die, Lear must be deprived of everything (especially, and finally, his beloved child), and Falstaff must be banished before we can understand how deeply we feel about them. But Prospero renounces his magic on his own terms, as part of his long-range plan, once it has accomplished his desired ends. He starts in control and he ends in control. (No wonder I find him difficult to warm to. I too have been accused, justly, of liking control too much, of creating my own little island in which I can rule supreme. And, as I said in regard to George Eliot, we always dislike most the flaws we possess ourselves.)

Shakespeare does, however, leave us some wiggle room. If *The Tempest* is about power, it is also about equality in the face of power, equality undermining power. We get a strong hint of this in the opening scene, the "tempest" itself, when Gonzalo, the king's councilor, is talking to the Boatswain over the ever-increasing roar of the storm. Each man is doing his job: Gonzalo is counseling, and the Boatswain is trying to save the vessel from shipwreck, a job made more difficult by the intrusive presence of the passengers. "You mar our labor. Keep your cabins; you do assist the storm," he points out to Gonzalo and his companions.

Gonzalo: Nay, good, be patient.
Boatswain: When the sea is. Hence! What cares these roarers for the name of king? To cabin! Silence! Trouble us not!
Gonzalo: Good, yet remember whom thou hast aboard.
Boatswain: None that I more love than myself.

On the one hand, this is a perfectly straightforward state-ment, an attempt at reasonable reassurance—the Boatswain is already doing his best to save the ship because his own life is at stake. But it is also treasonous, or ironic (or both): one isn't supposed to value oneself as much as one's king. Gon-zalo responds by saying to his fellow courtiers: "I have great comfort from this fellow. Methinks he hath no drowning mark upon him; his complexion is perfect gallows." I thought this was a hilarious line, but since there is no evi-dence elsewhere in the play that Gonzalo has a sense of humor (he is as sententious as Polonius, and W. H. Auden accurately describes him as "good but stupid"), he probably didn't intend it to be funny. Which doesn't mean it isn't funny: the late romances are very strange in the way they use humor, and we often feel we are laughing in the wrong place, just before something terrible happens. (A prime ex-ample is the famous stage direction "Exit pursued by a bear." Auden thinks this means *The Winter's Tale* is unactable

— "Some of it just has to be read. On stage, unfortunately, the exit of Antigonus, *'pursued by a bear,'* is too funny" — but that seems to me to overlook all the other places in these two late plays where Shakespeare provokes us into an outburst of uncomfortable laughter.)

The Boatswain's insistence on loving himself as much as a king — on equality, if you will — simmers on, in the course of the play, as a form of tension between the feeling called love and the realities of power, or hierarchy, or control. This time through, I was made particularly uncomfortable by the way Prospero masterminds the love affair between his daughter and the king's son. Can Miranda and Ferdinand really be said to be falling in love, in the way we usually like to think of that emotion, if Prospero is so actively pulling the puppet-strings? It's like *A Midsummer Night's Dream,* but taken seriously: the drug lasts for the rest of a lifetime. Miranda, also, struck me as rather dippy this time, a Dickensian female posing as a smart chess-playing princess, or (what would be even worse) a smart chess-player posing as a weak Dickensian female so as not to scare off her less intelligent suitor. Coleridge calls her Shakespeare's "favorite character" — in this one play, I assume he means, but still, not a conclusion I would ever have drawn. I don't see how the man who invented the marvelous Cleopatra or the witty Beatrice or the smart Portia or even the bravely parent-defying Desdemona and Juliet could really be fond of a self-abasing girl who says things to her lover like:

> I am your wife, if you will marry me;
> If not, I'll die your maid. To be your fellow
> You may deny me; but I'll be your servant,
> Whether you will or no.

She is a logical result of the Prospero School of Authoritarian Education, which, when it does not produce rebellion like Caliban's, produces subservience like Miranda's.

Is it love that Ferdinand and Miranda feel for each other, or is it just a reaction to Prospero's clever staging? The play asks this about everything important (love, knowledge, power, magic, art): Is it real, or not? And what would "real" mean, anyway, in a play? *The Tempest* causes us to doubt the evidence of our senses, and at the same time allows us to enjoy that doubt, though the enjoyment is, admittedly, laced with darker fears. The play seals us, temporarily, into a safe theatrical space where we can afford doubt, where it may even become something useful and benign.

The Winter's Tale is something of an opposite case: doubt run rampant, a bottomless pit of doubt, terrifying and engulfing doubt. The point, as Auden eloquently put it in his 1947 lectures on Shakespeare, is that "you can't prove that a person loves you, you can't prove that you shouldn't distrust someone. Once doubt is raised in Leontes' mind, it becomes almost an *acte gratuit*. He embraces doubt as a certainty."

Leontes' conversion from a confident husband to a doubting one is so instantaneous it is almost ludicrous. He jovially urges Hermione to help him persuade their guest Polixenes to stay longer with them, but no sooner has she done so than he suspiciously observes the way his wife and his best friend are "paddling palms and pinching fingers," and suddenly he is convinced they are having an affair. The transformation is so abrupt that we can hardly believe it; as you read the page or two in question, it feels as if Leontes has had some kind of psychotic break. But, as with *The Tempest,* good actors would be able to make the scene credible and even wrenching. Hermione and Polixenes probably ought to be flirting with each other slightly, the way opposite halves of a married-couple foursome tend to do. (Leontes, that is, should not be hallucinating, but misinterpreting.) And Leontes himself must be a terrifically complex figure, someone who can make us despise him, fear him, and pity him all at once. As he entertains the idea of Hermione's unfaithfulness, Leontes is playing with his little boy, Mamillius, and this scene needs to be heartbreaking in all sorts of ways. We need to feel how much he loves his son so that we can, first of all, sense the terrible violation and self-violation entailed in depriving the child of his mother, and, even more, so we can measure the seriousness of the blow to Leontes when he learns his son has died.

Like so many important events in this play—Antigonus's annihilation by the bear, for instance, or Hermione's sixteen years in hiding—the little prince's death occurs offstage. Leontes is in the midst of his most hateful, irrational rant. He has refused to listen to the good sense of Hermione's lady-in-waiting, Paulina; he has declined to believe Hermione's own honest eloquence; and he has even denied the evidence brought to him at his request from Delphi. It's not as if the signs were at all unclear, either: the message from Apollo's oracle reads: "Hermione is chaste, Polixenes blameless, Camillo a true subject, Leontes a jealous tyrant . . ." Not too much room for misinterpretation *there*. Just as the king willfully and outrageously counters the oracle with "This is mere falsehood," a servant enters from offstage and announces,

> O sir, I shall be hated to report it.
> The prince your son, with mere conceit and fear
> Of the queen's speed, is gone.

"How gone?" asks Leontes. "Is dead," the servant clarifies.

Shakespeare offers no stage directions here. (He rarely did—that's one of the reasons "pursued by a bear" is so noteworthy, and so unignorable.) Later editors have inserted a *"Hermione swoons"* and an eventual *"Exeunt Paulina and Ladies with Hermione"* to accord with the developing plot, but even they have not thought of any directions for Leontes. How could they? His behavior at this point is impossible to describe, much less comprehend, for he seems to turn on a dime from vicious irrationality to sane remorsefulness. The first words out of his mouth, after he hears of his son's death, are "Apollo's angry, and the heavens themselves / Do strike at my injustice." Does he pause between the terrible news and his devastated response? He must. There would have to be complete silence onstage while Leontes took in the full implications of what he had brought about. Perhaps he would respond physically to the terrible blow, or perhaps he would remain still; I don't know. I do know that it would all be up to the actor playing Leontes—he, and he alone, could make this moment work.

The reason this scene is so important (and I have only noticed this now, on this reading) is that the child's death is the first and most extreme of the irreparable losses in the play. Up to now, it has all been reversible. Until this moment, we can't be sure whether we are watching a comedy about jealousy or a tragedy about jealousy—whether we are in *Much Ado About Nothing*, say, or *Othello*. As it turns out, we are in neither, but in some strange, hybrid world where terrible things happen alongside lovely and amusing ones. A world, that is, very much like our own.

Before this moment, Leontes has said and done horrible things to Hermione, but they are all on the level of insult rather than injury. They could all, given the proper conditions, be retracted, apologized for, made good. When you have been married for only a few years (as Hermione and Leontes probably have at this point—their first child is still quite small), you might imagine that anger and insult are irrevocable. But after a few more years, if you manage to stay together, you may well begin to think otherwise. Almost everything that takes place on the level of insult falls outside the category of "unforgivable," and the longer you are married, the more likely you are to understand this. The question asked by *The Winter's Tale* is how much that category can be shrunk—how much the seemingly unforgivable can be made, if not exactly forgivable, then subject to mutual kindness and lack of ultimate recrimination.

Reading *The Winter's Tale* this time, I realized two important things about myself. One is that I have cautiously guided my life by the principle of *avoiding irreparable loss.* This is not to say that I am cautious about everything. In my work life, for instance, I have been flamboyantly unconventional in some ways, and I certainly have not been careful about accumulating money. It's also true that, principles or no, you can only guard yourself against loss to a certain extent, and beyond that point luck plays a major part. In that respect I have, so far, been lucky. But it's also true that I act, overall, in a manner designed to minimize regret. If I look back on all the decisions in my life, I do not see even one major cause for regret. This is both the best and the worst thing I can say about myself. My desire to avoid loss has kept me on the straight and narrow; I have not consciously let myself in for anything that contained, at the front end, a huge potential for regret. And that has been a limiting principle, I now see, as well as a useful and soothing one.

The other thing I realized, as a result of *The Winter's Tale,* is that I have almost no capacity for forgiveness. I don't easily forgive myself (that's one of the reasons I have to avoid occasions for regret), and I don't like to forgive others or have them forgive me. This is not to say that I believe in holding long-term grudges. On the contrary, I, who otherwise have a very good memory, will sometimes be surprised to learn that I have had a falling-out with someone in the distant past. I will have to be reminded, when we meet again, that some incident or other prevented us from speaking for years. And this will be equally true whether I committed the atrocity or the other person did—in either case, the unpleasantness in my mind will have seeped away over time. But through forgetting rather than forgiving.

It's not just that I am not good at forgiveness. It's also that I actively dislike it, as a mode of human relations. It seems to me excessively Christian—that is, it seems to posit some alliance with a sin-cleansing god, some effort on the part of the forgiving individual to act in a godlike manner. To my ear, there is nothing so insulting as the line "I forgive you," because it presumes that the speaker has the right to forgive. This is not to say that I don't believe in apologies—I do, very sincerely. Apologies are human. But forgiveness is divine, and I don't believe in divinity.

Leontes' terrible behavior is the direct cause of several irreparable losses. First and foremost is the little prince's death. Then there is the death of Antigonus in the wilds of Bohemia, where he has been sent to get rid of Leontes' and Hermione's new baby, Perdita. We are reminded of Antigonus's death in the very last speeches of the play, after Leontes has been reunited with his queen through the good offices of Paulina, Antigonus's widow. As she sees Leontes and Hermione together, Paulina falls into a moment of self-pity (or perhaps it's a self-mocking imitation of self-pity), saying,

> I, an old turtle,
> Will wing me to some withered bough and there
> My mate, that's never to be found again,
> Lament till I am lost.

To which Leontes—the man solely responsible for her husband's death—has the nerve, the outright gall, to respond:

> O peace, Paulina!
> Thou shouldst take a husband by my consent,
> As I by thine a wife. This is a match . . .

Hardly a match, I would say: he lost her husband, she found his wife. But this imbalance is so obvious that Leontes must be aware of it. So this bit of dialogue between the king and

Paulina becomes something else entirely: an unspoken acknowledgment of the irreversible harm he's done her and the infinite good she's done him in return. Her self-pity is both real and self-mocking, and so is his response, because Paulina and Leontes know each other well enough and care for each other deeply enough to joke about serious things.

The other loss that can never be made good, in this play, is the sixteen years of Perdita's life that her mother will never retrieve. Hermione has her daughter back in the end, but only as a young woman on the verge of marriage; the baby, the small child, and the growing girl are gone forever, vanished as if in the twinkling of an eye. (In the play, sixteen years pass between acts, which seems unrealistic until you start to think about where *your* last sixteen years have gone.) Nor does the play, even in the midst of its final happiness, allow us to forget this loss. Hermione's only lines in the last act are spoken about Perdita, and to her:

> You gods, look down
> And from your sacred vials pour your graces
> Upon my daughter's head! Tell me, mine own,
> Where hast thou been preserved? where lived? how found
> Thy father's court?

The queen has come back to Leontes as a wife, and she is clearly ready to love him again (or love him still): "She embraces him," "She hangs about his neck," the witnesses to their reunion report. But she says nothing about forgiveness, to him or to anyone else. Is this because she feels there is "No cause, no cause," as Cordelia said to Lear when he tried to apologize for *his* terrible behavior? I think not. Forgiveness belongs to the world of the tragedies. Something else—not forgetfulness, but its clearheaded, clear-eyed opposite—is required here, if life is to go on with anything resembling happiness. The scene in which Hermione's statue comes to life (a moment that should bring tears to the audience's eyes if it's done properly onstage) is always called the "reconcilia-tion" scene, not the "forgiveness" scene. Perhaps the oppo-site of forgetfulness is reconciliation.

The Winter's Tale is a play full of gaps—not only the huge gap in time between the third and fourth acts, but also the many absences, spaces, and silences that leave us wondering how and why something happened. The largest of these, in a dramatic sense, is the absence of any explanation whatso-ever for how Hermione came to be hidden in Paulina's house, ready to be revealed as a statue. In a normal, sub-Shakespearean play, we would get a behind-the-scenes scene showing us the conferences between Hermione and Paulina, with references to Hermione's supposed death and subse-quent recovery, the preparation of the "statue," Leontes' cur-rent state of mind, and so on; we might even get a full ex-planation after the fact, delivered as if to Leontes and his courtiers, to explain how the trick was managed. We get none of this. The last we heard of Hermione, she was dead and buried. Now we see her as a statue, and then she comes to life. We learn, at the exact moment when Leontes learns (or perhaps a few seconds before), that she is not dead after all. This is Shakespeare's gift to us, and it is what brings tears to our eyes. At least a part of what we considered irreparably lost is being restored to us, and at such a moment we are in no mood to ask for explanations. We simply accept the granting of our wish.

The Tempest, in contrast, is a relatively seamless play, with no gaps of this sort. There is, to begin with, no temporal gap at all. In fact, it is the only play of Shakespeare's that pre-serves the classical unities of time, space, and action—"which accounts for Prospero's long, expository narrative at the beginning of the play instead of action," comments Auden, who then adds: "Maybe he made a bet with Ben Jon-son about whether he could do it or not." It is a shaped and shapely play; "perfect" is a word that critics sometimes apply to it, because it has the balance and cohesion of a circle. Part of the reason there is no gap is that it encloses us in that circle as well, reaching out to our reality—the reality of being in a theater—and making that part of the play.

They are very different, these two late works of Shakespeare's, and yet each requires of us something I didn't have when I read them the first time. I know I didn't understand them then, because I didn't love them; it's as simple as that. A great deal of time had to pass (Hermione's lost sixteen years and more) before I could bring to each play the thing that would make me feel it as complete. In the case of *The Tempest*, it was my experience in the theater, my months and years of observing and caring about performances. And in the case of *The Winter's Tale*, it was my life—all *those* months and years. The gaps in *The Winter's Tale* are there for a very good reason. We fill them with ourselves.

THE TREE
OF KNOWLEDGE

~~~

S INCE *Paradise Lost* is,
among other things, about the acquisition of knowledge, it is
fitting that I associate the poem with three teachers who
were very important to me. Two of these teachers were people I knew; one was a critic I met only through the pages of
his books. It's probable that all three would have been important to me anyway, as influences on my way of thinking
and feeling and writing about literature. But it's also possible that their connection with this amazing poem (which
also amazes as a drama and a novel and a philosophical
work) has strengthened my allegiance to them. Did they
make me care so much for the poem, or did *it* make me care
so much for their teaching? The question itself, with its de-
pendence on reversal, partakes of the very sensibility and
texture of *Paradise Lost*. Apparently my mind has been so
shaped by that texture (or perhaps, to invoke another Mil-
tonic alternative, my mind was so receptive to that sensibility in the first place) that I can barely tell anymore where it
leaves off and I begin.

I will come back eventually to the strangeness of this—
the fact that an atheistic, rebellious female should be so smit-
ten by a poem that, on its surface, advocates Christianity,
obedience, and the submission of women. The word "advocates," for instance, will warrant a closer look: if Milton was
a lawyer, as so many critics suggest, he was certainly not the
normal kind that defends only one side at a time. But for
now let me speak about the teachers.

The first was Christopher Ricks, whom I've already mentioned. I didn't study *Paradise Lost* with him—I didn't study
Paradise Lost at all, until I came to Berkeley as a graduate student—but I certainly knew, from quite early on in our
friendship, that his first book was called *Milton's Grand Style.*
I evidently acquired this book well before reading Milton;
the Penguin bookmark that fell out of it when I opened it the
other day indicates that I bought it in England sometime in
the early 1970s. Though I may not have read it thoroughly at
the time (the bookmark, I confess, fell out of the *middle* of the
book), I had absorbed a great deal of its method through the
man himself. That there was such a thing as great line-by-
line poetry even in a book-length work like *Paradise Lost;* that
these local effects all furthered the larger purpose of the
poem; that Milton could at times reasonably be compared to
Hopkins: these were things I already believed on first encountering Milton's epic. And the way the argument was
made—the capacious knowledge about previous critics and
editors, the knife-sharp ability to make fine distinctions, and,
above all, the ever-present insistence on fairness—these too
were strategies I had been amply exposed to, even if I had
not fully managed to convert them into my own.

I see this now. What I saw then was the extent to which
Christopher and I disagreed on at least one major point, the
character of Eve. He took what I considered the traditional
Christian line on the guilt of Woman and had no trouble
placing most of the blame for the Fall on her. Her evident
charm Christopher disdained as "pert vivacity," and her

speech about wanting to work independently of Adam struck him as a "grave presentation of Eve's self-will." He even insisted that "for Eve to be wrong about anything (even that she would soon be back) is for her to be wrong about everything." This seemed a little harsh to me then, and still does. There is more modulation in Milton's view of Eve— more modulation, and more affection.

Affection for Eve *without* modulation was what I got from my second teacher, Edward Snow. It was with Ed that I first went through Milton's poem in detail, in a seminar devoted wholly to *Paradise Lost*, and it was Ed's enthusiasm for the work that initially sparked my own. His version was totally other than the traditional one, and far more congenial to the atheist female. In his view, this supposedly Christian poem was actually a commemoration of the pagan myths so plentifully mentioned in it, and it was also a celebration of the rebellious Eve.

Ed Snow was the kind of English professor that female students adored—not just because of looks or charm, but because he made women the heroes of everything. As he saw it, Juliet was insuperably wiser than Romeo, Cleopatra was far more attractive than Antony, Vermeer's women were more intimately in touch with their world than the men around them could ever be, and even Bruegel's girls, as pictured in *Children's Games*, were more adventurous and inventive than their masculine playmates. Nor did this stance seem in any way a false position, a hypocritical way to garner the approval of women. Ed truly believed that women— at least literary, artistic, and cinematic portrayals of women —were superior to men. And this attitude, in his case, was interestingly *not* combined with the sort of soft, feckless, long-haired, fuzzy-edged personality found in the stereotypically "sensitive" man of that era. On the contrary, Ed was excessive, insistent, and irritable. He defended his heroines with passion, and he could be unpedagogically scathing when a student said something he considered stupid or wrong. His irritation sprang from allegiance: he treated *Paradise Lost*, or any other artwork he truly cared about, as if it were a living reality, something worthy of emotional respect and intense visceral response. He would yell at us if we used the word "Milton" in class—as in "I think Milton believes . . ."—because he wanted us to see the characters as something larger than mere allegorical placeholders in an individual author's argument. And I also think, now, that he banned Milton's name because he had trouble believing (just as Satan had trouble believing about God) that any single being, however powerful and wise, could be capable of so much astonishing creation. For Ed, *Paradise Lost* transcended its maker just as surely as Satan, Eve, and Adam transcended theirs.

The bridge between Ed's view and Christopher's—between the passionate defense of the characters' emotional reality and the lucid, informed attention to the lines of Milton's poetry—came, for me, in the form of William Empson. He was my third teacher, the one I never met (though, late in Empson's life and early in mine, I witnessed from afar one of his lectures on Andrew Marvell). Many people consider *Milton's God* his craziest book, but to me it remains his most useful and compelling. Rereading it, I am reminded of how much my own ideal of the critic's role has been formed by Empson. I could do a whole chapter on his autobiographical asides, which are as delicately worded and as charmingly digressive as Orwell's, though they reveal a personality far more vulnerable and open than anything Orwell was ever willing to show us. But let me instead, to give the flavor of both his passion and his erudition, quote from a long passage about the job of criticism:

> A curious trick has been played on modern readers here; they are told: "Why, but of course you must read the poem taking for granted that Milton's God is good; not to do that would be absurdly unhistorical. Why, the first business of a literary

critic is to sink his mind wholly into the mental world of the author, and in a case like this you must accept what they all thought way back in early times." I think this literary doctrine is all nonsense anyhow; a critic ought to use his own moral judgement, for what it is worth, as well as try to understand the author's, and that is the only way he can arrive at a "total reaction." But in a case like this the argument is also grossly unhistorical. No doubt Milton would have snorted if a Victorian had come up and praised him for making Satan good, but anyone who told him he had made God wicked would find his mind surprisingly at home; there would be some severe cross-questioning (is this a Jesuit or merely an Arminian?), but if that passed off all right he would ask the visitor to sit down and discuss the point at length.

Christopher Ricks loved William Empson, and it was through him that I first came to care for this marvelous critic, but on *Paradise Lost* I think Empson actually comes down closer to Ed Snow. Here he is, for instance, on the question of Eve's motives:

> She thinks: "The reason why all the males keep on saying I mustn't eat the apple, in this nerve-wracking way, is obviously that they are longing to have me do it; this is the kind of thing they need a queen to have the nerve to do"; so she does it . . . In effect, she presumes that God will love her for eating the apple, at any rate later on, when he has realized that that was what he had wanted her to do at bottom. So he would have done if he had been better.

For Empson, the basis of the poem is that God is a pretty horrible character, and its interest derives from the way Milton honestly and intelligently faces up to that fact, though with reluctance and without giving up his attempt to "justify the ways of God to men."

. . .

More than any other book I've discussed—more even than *Don Quixote*—*Paradise Lost* offers a first reading that is already a rereading. Almost nobody who has read this poem in English (except, possibly, Empson's Chinese and Japanese students) has done so without knowing the story beforehand. The endpoint toward which the plot is tending, and even the exact language of the Fall (a scene Milton borrows nearly wholesale from the King James version of Genesis), are inalterably engraved in our collective memories. The problem Milton sets himself is to give us this fixed story and make us imagine it as not fixed, but open. To persuade us of Adam and Eve's free will (a concept on which God harps frequently and annoyingly throughout the poem), the author of *Paradise Lost* needs to create in us the sense that the Fall is occurring once again, at this minute, as we are reading about it —that the act of eating the apple, though foreseen in advance, is not actually done until we see it done. To a certain extent this is the problem faced by all authors of narrative fiction or even nonfiction: we readers must feel that the characters have an ongoing life of their own even though we know, with another part of our minds, that the words have long since been set down on the page. But in Milton's case the problem of "suspense," if you will, has been grossly exacerbated by two additional difficulties. He is stuck with a story we already know; and he is stuck with an all-powerful character who knows everything before it happens, and yet who claims to have no responsibility for other people's behavior.

All this I knew when I read *Paradise Lost* the first time. In fact, I am astonished to discover what I knew then. Reading through the papers I wrote for Ed Snow (don't worry, I'm not going to inflict them on you), I find all kinds of arcane data and cleverly remarked correspondences—sources unearthed, crucial lines memorized, previous critics answered, linguistic ambiguities teased out, all that sort of thing. This is

the opposite case to *Don Quixote,* which I once read inno-
cently and now read knowledgeably. With *Paradise Lost* I
have moved to that Lethean condition beyond knowledge,
where all my once-treasured information has been washed
away. Faint echoes of it surface here and there, in well-
remembered lines like "Hesperian fables true, / If true, here
only—and of delicious taste" or "In shadier bower / More
sacred and sequestered, though but feigned, / Pan or Sylva-
nus never slept, nor Nymph / Nor Faunus haunted," which
for me are still haunted by their underlying pagan myths.
But for the most part this reading is more natural, more
fluid, less weighted down with analytic attention than my
earlier one was. And having less of a case to make, I am less
concerned to dispute or engage or expose or applaud Milton's case. I read the poem less as if it were a legal brief and
more as if it were a novel—though, granted, a deeply philosophical novel, a work as fascinated by its own methods of
communicating the story as by the story itself.

At first, in this rereading, I noticed those methods in a
rather distracted and piecemeal way, as if they were mere
tics of the author, strange little habits he happened to engage
in. There is Milton's excessive love of inversion, for instance
(you can hear it even in the two passages I just quoted),
which places the verb very late in the sequence, puts the adjective after the noun, and in general twists the whole sentence glaringly out of the usual English word order. Then
there's the interest he evidently takes in what I would call
the mechanics of things: the metallurgical architecture of
Hell, the details of angelic digestion and angelic sex, the various kinds of flowers grown in Heaven and in Paradise, the
precise way a snake moved before it was cursed into crawl-
ing, the engineering of the bridge that spanned the abyss between our world and Death's realm, and so on. This set of in-
terests leads into the more specific question of how things
are created. Milton is intrigued by the whole idea of preg-

nancy, and creation, and of course The Creation. An image that beautifully brings all three of these notions together is the one of the animals being conjured out of the ground on the sixth day of creation:

> The grassy clods now calved; now half appeared
> The tawny lion, pawing to get free
> His hinder parts — then springs, as broke from bonds,
> And rampant shakes his brinded mane.

It looks great, in the mind's-eye movie, and it also *sounds* great; surely even Hopkins couldn't manage a better sprung rhythm than "then springs, as broke from bonds."

It is Adam's job to name all these newly created beasts, and here I found myself focusing on the philosophical question Milton raises about this process: Does Adam actually give the animals their names, or does he simply guess their names correctly? "I bring them to receive / From thee their names," God says to him in Book VIII, and then a few pages later compliments him on having "rightly named" them, as if to say that Adam accurately perceived the cow-ness or lion-ness inherent in each one. This question about the origin of words — do they come from God, or not? — is linked to, though not the same as, Satan's persistent question about his own origins. Is God really, as he alleges, the creator of everything, and could there actually have been a time before he, Satan, existed? This is not just the child's question about where he comes from (and the child's doubt about the truth of the bizarre explanation); it is also a very rational, adult effort to come to grips with paradox. How can a "world without end" have had a beginning, and how can there be a "before" and an "after" in eternity, where time itself is measureless?

Doubts about what God has done and what he means by it are not just the province of Satan in this poem. We are meant to have them too, if we are to enter fully into the experience of understanding how the Fall came about. If Milton expected us simply to take the gospel truths on faith, he would never have bothered to write the poem. He is engaged in an "Argument" (as the prose headpiece to each of the twelve books is called), and the presence of argument indicates that there are at least two credible sides.

What strikes me most forcefully, this time through, is how very well he argues Eve's side. By the time she bites the apple, the act seems not only plausible but rational. She has consistently been referred to, both in her absence and in her hearing, as intellectually and morally inferior to Adam; yet Adam has made clear, to her and to God, that he wants an equal partner. (That's why he's not satisfied just to be the sole superior being surrounded by inferior beasts, though God himself claims to find such an existence satisfactory.) If the fruit from the Tree of Knowledge has made the previously mute snake speak so persuasively, wouldn't it work wonders on a human female, making her at least the intellectual equal of her husband and therefore, by his own definition, a more lovable mate? And wouldn't the additional knowledge make both her and Adam more like angels—in that sense, closer to God? Of course, the snake could be lying. But if he can't be trusted, if even *one* liar can make his way into Paradise, why should she assume that Raphael's warning against eating the apple was reliable? The two pieces of advice—the snake's and Raphael's—conflict, so one or the other has to be wrong, but only additional knowledge can help her out of the dilemma. The Tree is offering her that knowledge.

(Nor is this offer a mere trick. The apple does have a tangible effect on Eve's perceptions, as we learn in the passage immediately following her first taste:

> such delight till then, as seemed,
> In fruit she never tasted, whether true,

> Or fancied so through expectation high
> Of knowledge; nor was Godhead from her thought.

This reminds me of nothing so much as Wordsworth's Immortality Ode, with its sense of a deep connection with one's present, felt reality, which is also a felt connection with God. It would be too weird to suggest that Eve, in biting the apple, made way for the gratefully religious moments of inspiration that Wordsworth was able to have in childhood and youth—as if, until we were actually separated from God, we couldn't bask in that unusual degree of connection with him —but something of that feeling is certainly at work here.)

At this point, admiring how cunningly Milton has constructed the plot, I begin to realize that *Paradise Lost* does not just resemble *any* novel; it reminds me, very specifically, of a mystery novel. Or rather, it reminds me of the strategies a mystery writer must use in order to make the plot compelling to us. He starts at the end and works backward, laying his groundwork as he goes, and then we move forward along the same path, picking up the clues and marveling at the neatness of the outcome. And like a good mystery writer, Milton injects his clues so delicately, so invisibly, that we are not aware of why we are being told certain things until much later, when they come to mean something to us.

John Buchan, in the first chapter of his novel *The Three Hostages*, shows us how it's done. The conversation is between the narrator, Richard Hannay, and a visiting Dr. Greenslade:

> The doctor picked up a detective novel I had been reading, and glanced at the title page.
>
> "I can read most things," he said, "but it beats me how you waste time over such stuff. These shockers are too easy, Dick. You could invent better ones for yourself."
>
> "Not I. I call that a dashed ingenious yarn. I can't think how the fellow does it."
>
> "Quite simple. The author writes the story inductively, and

the reader follows it deductively. Do you see what I mean?"

"Not a bit," I replied.

"Look here. I want to write a shocker, so I begin by fixing on one or two facts which have no sort of obvious connection."

"For example?"

"Well, imagine anything you like. Let us take three things a long way apart"—He paused for a second to consider—"say, an old blind woman spinning in the Western Highlands, a barn in a Norwegian *saeter*, and a little curiosity shop in North London kept by a Jew with a dyed beard. Not much connection between the three? You invent a connection—simple enough if you have any imagination, and you weave all three into the yarn. The reader, who knows nothing about the three at the start, is puzzled and intrigued, and, if the story is well arranged, finally satisfied. He is pleased with the ingenuity of the solution, for he doesn't realize that the author fixed on the solution first, and then invented a problem to suit it."

But what gives the added turn to this screw, what lends the real thrill to this thriller, is the fact that these three "random" things turn out to be the essential clues in John Buchan's novel. (Talk about vertigo. I'm sure I could have done a whole chapter on Buchan's Richard Hannay books, which continue to grab me each time I reread them, at intervals of ten or fifteen years. But my book, unlike Milton's, is not capacious enough to include all the possibilities.)

Of course, one crucial difference between *Paradise Lost* and *The Three Hostages* is that Milton doesn't get to "invent" his problem and his solution; he is stuck with the ones in the record. But something similar is at work in the nature of the thrill. In both of these books, the author is letting us in on his own strategy in order to make it pertinent to the content of his tale. He wants us to see how the trick works and then be tricked anyway. That we can still be fooled, even after being warned, is part of the point, part of the suspense. And who,

in *Paradise Lost*, is the figure closest to the detective-story author? Why, God, naturally, who sees everything at once, and
for whom thinking backward, from the future to the past, is
second nature. The problem set for the solver of the mystery
(who can be Milton, or Eve, or Satan, or us) is to learn to
think like God—to have all of eternity envisioned simultaneously, so that forward and backward, inductive and de-
ductive, potential and actual become indifferentiable.

A surprising number of the inconsistencies and eccentricities in the plot of *Paradise Lost* become much more logical
once you adopt this God's-eye view of time. Take the naming of the animals, for example. Milton doesn't even have to
posit that Adam has any special insight, or foresight, for the
given name to turn out to be the same as the right name. All
we need to remember is that God has known all along exactly what Adam will call each animal. For God, the moment
when he thought of creating a lion and the moment when
Adam called it "lion" are both eternally available—both simultaneous, if you will—so there is no gap between Adam's
word and his own divine conception of the thing.

The interest in mechanics, too, is part of that all-seeing,
time-blurring approach. For God (and, by extension, for Milton), how something was put together and what it is now are
not chronologically separable qualities: each thing shows its
history, its engineering, in its finished state. This is as true for
Gardens of Eden as it is for epic poems, and indeed the moment in *Paradise Lost* when Milton seems to feel most
warmly toward his difficult client is when God admires his
handiwork at the end of the sixth day:

> how it showed
> In prospect from his throne, how good, how fair,
> Answering his great idea.

This maker's pride in a complicated concept beautifully exe-
cuted is something the poet can understand, and so can we

all, if we think about any piece of work we've accomplished well. (I had forgotten, by the way, until I read *Paradise Lost* this time, that labor predates the expulsion. Work can count as a pleasure, that is, and not just as a punishment. As I noted with my newly developed attention to gardening, Adam and Eve labor daily among their vegetables and flowers before the Fall. And even God works hard; otherwise, manifestly, he would not need a day of rest.)

Milton's adoption of God's sense of time also helps explain those inverted sentences. In this extraordinary realm where we can move backward and forward along all eternity, we can also move forward and backward at the sentence level, and so reading—something that is normally one-way—develops an extra dimension. By making us take in last things first, Milton's inverted style asks us to become like God, keeping the whole picture in mind at every moment and reinterpreting the present in light of what follows it. Yet the style also has an undeniable forward motion, a directional urgency; we are human, after all, and we mark our lives with endpoints. This is perhaps the chief advantage that accrues to Milton along with the many disadvantages of a fixed story: we know where we are going and we know when we have arrived there, and there is a certain satisfaction to having reached the inevitable. This is true on the plot level, naturally, but it is also apparent in the sentences, as Christopher Ricks aptly remarks. "When a sentence surges forward like that," he says in *Milton's Grand Style,* "the end of it seems less a destination than a destiny."

To write the way God thinks seems a very large ambition indeed, but *Paradise Lost* is nothing if not ambitious. The poem repeatedly calls attention to its own ambitiousness, as if we would be in danger of missing it if Milton didn't point it out to us. Milton may not have identified himself with Satan, or with Eve, but he certainly went very far in risking that *we* would so identify him. The two qualities of his poem that he never lets us forget—the godlike ambition behind its aim and the vast amount of knowledge behind its execution —are exactly the ones that cost us the Garden of Eden. You could say that Milton is simply making the best of a bad bargain. Or you could say that he's reveling in what we came away with.

The one beautiful inconsistency that doesn't disappear from *Paradise Lost*, no matter how much of a godlike time scheme you try to adopt, is the sense of Milton's commitment to our earthly forms of knowledge, which are based on personal experience, public argument, and humanly transmitted learning. Empson cites Tillyard's observation that "if Milton had been in the Garden, he would have eaten the apple at once and written a pamphlet to prove that it was his duty." He did in fact write such a pamphlet, and it was called *Areopagitica.* In that defense of a free press in England, which was also an attack on the tyranny of censorship, Milton asked Parliament a question he considered rhetorical: "what wisdom can there be to choose, what continence to forbear without the knowledge of evil?" In other words, how could God have said that Adam and Eve possessed free will when he had forbidden them the necessary concomitant, a knowledge of good and evil? Milton gets himself out of this tight spot by prefacing his rhetorical question with the proviso "As therefore the state of man now is"—that is, after the Fall. In Paradise, apparently, all the usual bets were off, and God's strange rules prevailed.

But Milton cannot so easily rid himself of his earthly allegiance, either in his pamphlet or in *Paradise Lost* itself. We feel him straining against *that* tyranny too, even as he is trying to justify it. And finally it is the strain, the resistance, the inability to collapse himself into God's will, that makes the poem so enduringly powerful. If this is what it means to be fallen, we needn't entirely regret the Fall. No, need is not really the issue; we *cannot* regret it, because we have become something other than what we were at the time of our creation. We owe tremendous gratitude to those who made us, but there comes a time when we must use what they gave us to turn against them — to turn into our own flawed selves. That is what it means to grow up.

McEWAN IN TIME

I N 1992, in the pages of a national weekly magazine, I reviewed Ian McEwan's novel *Black Dogs*. I will spare you the entire review, but a few of its paragraphs will usefully lead us into my present subject:

> The world of a great novelist—and Ian McEwan is a great novelist—is continuous not only with our daily, lived world (from which, like Antaeus, he derives a large part of his strength), but also with the slightly distorted, hyper-real, eerily patterned but surprisingly free world he has populated with all his fictional characters. When he sits down to write a new novel, he returns again as a traveler to that world, and the novel is the letter he posts out to us . . .
>
> From the beginning, McEwan's world has been one in which sexual love holds both great allure and great peril; in which violence is a weapon of intimates; in which the self-enclosure of family life can be both comforting and terrifying; in which childhood deserves to be treasured but needs to be outgrown; in which innocence is a danger to itself and others;

in which one relies on the kindness of sometimes sinister strangers; in which time flows backward and forward, with last things influencing first as well as first last . . . It is a world where the horrifying, the sad, and the comic intermingle; and it is a world where fear and its henchman, suspense, generally play leading roles. One reviewer described McEwan's last book as the kind of novel which would result "if Stephen King could write like Henry James," and in a way this is true of all his books. The horror lies precisely in the delicate turn of the screw.

In each novel from *The Comfort of Strangers* onward, Mc-Ewan has been fiddling with the nature of suspense—that is, with the relationship between fear and time. *The Comfort of Strangers* is pure foreboding. We feel throughout that something awful is going to happen, and in the end it does. (If you have only seen the movie, forget it. Pinter's idiosyncratic screenplay flattens the texture of the novel, making morbid nonsense out of what seems compelling and inevitable in the book.) *The Child in Time* creates nearly unbearable suspense out of an incident that took place before the novel opened: that is, the abduction of the main character's three-year-old daughter. In *The Innocent*, McEwan locates most of the suspense within a historical *fait accompli*. By giving us a doomed love story set around the discovery of an Anglo-American spy tunnel in 1950s Berlin, he makes us fruitlessly hope for an outcome that actual history has already defeated. And now, in *Black Dogs*, Ian McEwan pushes the limits of suspense even further. After telling us at the beginning of the novel that its two main characters lived into the late 1980s, he asks us at the novel's end to feel suspense in regard to something that happened to them in 1946. He asks us, that is, to fear the past.

Okay, enough of 1992. I have quoted from the *Black Dogs* piece here because it marks a specific stage in my relation to Ian McEwan's work. When I wrote it, I knew him essentially the way I knew John le Carré or Saul Bellow, as words on a page. If I had met the actual person, it was only in passing, at a bookstore reading, perhaps. But since then I have come to know Ian McEwan—not well, exactly, but over time and with some degree of intimacy. I have had dinner with him, alone and with friends. I have listened to his detailed descriptions of a nightmarish marital breakup and have responded with the appropriate sympathetic remarks. I have quizzed him on his family background, his daily routines, his preferred recreations. I have talked with him about books —his own and those of other writers. I know a great deal more about Ian McEwan than I did in 1992, and the way I read his novels has probably changed as a result.

There are also other, more general changes that have taken place in the way I read. I would no longer, I think, call anyone "a great novelist." I might say, in a colloquial sort of way, that *Don Quixote* or *The Idiot* (or even *Anna Karenina*, though it didn't happen to grab me this time around) is a great novel, but I would be hesitant about transferring the adjective from the novel to the novelist, and this would be particularly true of a living novelist. This is not just because tastes—especially, it seems, my tastes—vary, though that is indeed true: I can no longer vouch for the eternity of my convictions about *any* writer. But it is also because the word "great" has by now hardened into a club with which to batter the relativists in the so-called Culture Wars. It no longer refers to any sense of subjective judgment. It has become allied with millennial lists, and irrevocable canons, and permanent absolutes. And since the whole premise underlying my present endeavor is that we change our relation to specific books over time, I would feel silly using an adjective that has been kidnapped by the Unchanging Monuments camp.

This is not to say that I side with those people (if any of them really exist) who assert that Shakespeare is no better than Classic Comics. I still believe in hierarchies of judgment, and I make them all the time. If someone asks me to recommend an author's best book, or the best among three authors, I will have no hesitation in doing so. It's just that I am now more aware, despite the emphatic nature of my pronouncements, how temporary such judgments can ultimately be. And I am also more aware of the way an author I would once have classified as second-rate — Arnold Bennett, say, or William Dean Howells — is capable of producing a book that I will read and reread with increasing pleasure over the course of a lifetime. So the whole rating system no longer makes the kind of sense it did to me when I was younger.

And if the dead authors can shift around in my esteem, imagine how much more likely this is with living ones. It is safer reading the dead: they aren't so liable to rock the boat of their own reputation (though Hemingway and Ellison, with their recently published unfinished manuscripts, have given it a good try). Conversely, it can be more exciting to read the living, because you are still in the midst of the story; you don't yet know the shape of the whole career. To those of us who love suspense, as readers of Ian McEwan novels are bound to do, the openendedness is part of the allure. We can never be exactly sure what he will do next.

With an artist who is contemporaneous with you (as McEwan, only four years older, is roughly contemporaneous with me), there is generally a specific moment in the career that marks this person out as *yours* — a moment when you recognize that this artist, whose life had previously just been running alongside yours, has significantly crossed paths with you. This might happen with the first work you encounter, as it did for me with the choreographer Mark Morris and his *L'Allegro, il Penseroso, ed il Moderato*. If you start observing the career from the beginning, however, the decisive moment is more likely to involve a somewhat later work. For example, it was Errol Morris's third film, *The Thin Blue Line*, that won me over to him completely, though I had been intrigued by the earlier *Vernon, Florida* and *Gates of Heaven*. And while I read with admiration Ian McEwan's first book, the short-story collection *First Love, Last Rites*, shortly after it came out in 1975 (it was given to me by the man I still refer to as "my English boyfriend," though we have not been a couple for over twenty-five years), it was not until *The Child in Time* that I became a McEwan addict—that is, someone who buys each new novel and reads it in a single uninterrupted sitting. It was to *The Child in Time*, therefore, that I returned for this rereading project.

I must have reread the novel once before, in preparation for that 1992 review of *Black Dogs*. So I deduce, at any rate, from the yellow slip of notes that was stuck inside the front cover when I picked up the book this time. I have no memory, though, of that diligent rereading. What I do remember, as intensely as if it had happened last month, is the experience of reading the book for the first time in 1987. No notes whatsoever were taken *that* time. I was rapt, spellbound, inhabited. The mother of a two-year-old, I read this novel about a lost three-year-old with unremitting, quivering attention, as if it were the unfolding story of my own life.

As, in some ways, it turned out to be. Not, thank god, in regard to that plot development of the lost child, though, come to think of it, there are even echoes there. Between my first reading of the novel and this latest one, I did briefly lose my son in a crowded public place. He must have been about seven, and the three of us—my husband, my son, and I—had just arrived back at San Francisco airport after a trip to Europe. I left my husband and son with the bags and struggled through the vast, crowded customs-and-immigration holding pen to find out which line we belonged in. By the time I struggled back, my son was gone.

My husband, whose way of dealing with crisis is to become preternaturally calm, assured me there was no real danger. We were in the most heavily policed and restricted environment in Northern California, outside of San Quentin. No one could get out without a passport, and we had our son's passport; no kidnapped child could go back (onto the plane) or forward (through the immigration lines), so our son *had* to be somewhere in this crowded room with us. In any case, my husband—who had never, I should mention, read *The Child in Time*—gave no credence to the kidnapper theory. Our son, he insisted, had simply wandered off and would be found eventually.

He was, but not before I went into my frantic mode (which is *my* way of dealing with a crisis): rushing madly about the room, buttonholing official and unofficial people alike, demanding that announcements be made over the inaudible public address system, becoming ever more tearful as I repeated, "My son is lost! Have you seen my little boy?" I must have frightened a lot of fellow passengers that day. In the end, without any assistance from others, my son wandered back into view. But for those few moments I knew exactly how McEwan's main character, Stephen Lewis, had felt in the crowded supermarket where his daughter disappeared. "Now he was taking long strides, bawling her name as he pounded the length of an aisle and headed once more for the door. Faces were turning toward him . . . His fear was too evident, too forceful, it filled the impersonal, fluorescent space with unignorable human warmth." I had been captured, five years before the fact, in Ian McEwan's prose.

This is not prophecy. It is not even coincidence, exactly, since most parents lose their children briefly, or briefly fear they have lost them, at some point in the children's lives. What it is, instead, is McEwan's canniness. He has drawn on an experience in which the commonplace meets up with the horrifying, so that we all recognize the first half of the experience and all fear the second.

As for the other ways *The Child in Time* forecast my story, these were more particular and mostly had to do with my opinions, my writing. Rereading the novel now, after thirteen years, I find that in the intervening time I have repeatedly borrowed from it. If I had any conscious memory of the passages in question, I would almost have to call it plagiarism. But I do not remember having read them in the first place. So this time through, when I come across a paragraph about giving money to beggars that observes, "There was no way out. The art of bad government was to sever the line between public policy and intimate feeling, the instinct for what was right," I feel a shock of rueful recognition; I said much the same thing in an essay I wrote about philanthropy two years after first reading *A Child in Time*. At about the same time, I was also writing a book about men looking at women through art—about, among other things, the male artist's attraction to and envy of female reproductiveness. And now, in *The Child in Time*, I read, "Women simply enclosed the space that men longed to penetrate. The men's hostility was aroused."

The problem is, I no longer believe even my own opinions about men and women and childbirth, much less Ian McEwan's. Possibly in reaction to the direction gender politics took in the 1990s, I have generally given up on all attempts to classify artists by sex. The whole approach seems to me outmoded, useless, even dangerous, in the sense that biological determinism is always potentially harmful to humans. I don't like the idea of men *or* women being put into predetermined boxes, and I certainly don't like the idea of the physical act of giving birth being used as some kind of moral or aesthetic pinnacle of achievement.

This, in turn, means that the end of *The Child in Time*, which hinges on a birth, has been pretty much ruined for me. Granted, I never liked the ending as much as the rest of the book. Even the first time through, I found the parents'—

or the author's—refusal to recognize the newborn child's sex coy and unbelievable (coy on the part of the author, unbelievable on the part of the parents). But I accepted the childbirth as an ending to Stephen and Julie's terrible trial because it was a reward rather than a punishment, and I was grateful to McEwan for doling it out. (I had seen, in *The Comfort of Strangers*, how he could do the opposite.) I also accepted it as utterly in keeping with the rest of the novel. The earlier refusal to specify the prime minister's gender, the emotional importance given to Stephen and Julie's bed, and Stephen's wonderful "delivery" of the truck driver (whom he extracts headfirst from a crushed lorry) are all recapitulated in this final scene. So by the time I reached the end, the first time around, I was willing enough to admire the author's skillful knitting-up of all the plot elements. This time through, though, I wanted something more psychologically credible.

Still, as Randall Jarrell once said, a novel is a prose work of some length that has something wrong with it, and *The Child in Time* can still appeal to me even if the end is not fully satisfying. After all, I am no longer reading the book for suspense. What continues to work for me, I find, is the way in which McEwan's novel addresses our relationship to time. In this respect, *The Child in Time* is more important to me than ever. You might even say that its time obsessions lie behind this book about rereading in much the way those other passages lay behind my writing of the late 1980s.

I had already noticed in 1992 that McEwan's is a world "in which time flows backward and forward, with last things influencing first as well as first last." But the easy word "flow" belies the strenuousness of the effort. For McEwan's characters, as for all of us, time moves aggressively and unstoppably forward. It is only by the greatest exertions of the imagination—individual memory conspiring with wish, daydream, and a certain amount of authorial plotting

—that his characters can ever get it to move backward. Even then, what they achieve is not so much a movement, a backward flow, as a single moment of connectedness with the past.

In *The Child in Time*, in particular, we are constantly reminded of our own life's one-wayness. Stephen Lewis is someone who is repeatedly "shaken by the commonplace of irreversible time." Though he is only in his late thirties, he is very conscious of the fact that he has aged into a specific kind of person: "In his mid-twenties it had seemed arbitrarily humorous that he should be a successful writer of children's books, for there were still many other things he might have become. These days he could not imagine being anything else." But the routine aging process is not the only thing that haunts him. For Stephen, who has gone through the terrible and unexpected tragedy of losing his daughter Kate to a kidnapper, there is a much more gruesome aspect to time's irreversibility. He is aware of the way each small choice or casual gesture—even the refusal to make such choices or gestures—carries in its train a whole future, eliminating all other possible futures. Thinking back in subsequent months and years about his decision to take Kate to the supermarket that morning, he "was to make efforts to reenter this moment, to burrow his way back through the folds between events, crawl between the covers, and reverse his decision. But time—not necessarily as it is, for who knows that, but as thought has constituted it—monomaniacally forbids second chances."

The novel as a whole is a working out of the extent to which that last sentence is and is not true. There are some kinds of second chances, it turns out, but they do not involve going strictly backward, exactly retracing one's steps. Almost like a scientific experiment, *The Child in Time* tests out the various ways in which one might try to reach backward in time, scrutinizing the degree to which any of them really work.

There is, first of all, the standard path of memory and daydream. Stephen spends many hours reflecting back on his own childhood—hours during which he is supposed to be attending to the proceedings of a government subcommittee on childcare to which he has been appointed. (When I once asked Ian McEwan why all these daydreams occurred during the committee meetings, he answered, "Because I had never served on a committee, so I had to figure out some other way to get through those scenes.") As a children's author, Stephen also puts his memories and youthful longings to practical use—though it is a profession he has adopted only by chance, and resistantly. In trying to persuade Stephen to publish his first novel, *Lemonade*, as a children's book, his editor Charles Darke advises, "This book is not for children, it's for a child, and that child is you. *Lemonade* is a message from you to a previous self which will never cease to exist." But Stephen, listening to this pitch, recalls his own rather dull childhood and thinks to himself, "If he were to send back a message now, it would be one of dour encouragement: things will improve—very slowly."

The difference between Stephen Lewis and Charles Darke is the difference between a man who is glad to have emerged from childhood (though he still has the occasional regressive wish to "burrow his way back" and "crawl between the covers") and a man who regrets, to the point of psychosis, the need to grow up. Charles, as his last name implies, has a secret side which ultimately takes over him: he imagines himself to be, and in some ways transforms himself into, a ten-year-old boy. This is one way, obviously, to travel back in time, but it is a way that patently doesn't work; by the end of the novel Charles Darke's psychological conflicts have killed him.

Charles talks seriously and Stephen thinks humorously about the idea of sending a message back to one's childhood, but the point is that such a message (as Jenny Diski piercingly realized) can be sent but never delivered. The communication is all one-way. We can recall and even address our child selves, but they can't hear us—can't alter their behavior to suit our present needs, can't be cheered up (or toned down) by what we've learned, can't react in any way to the adults we have become. Perhaps this is why we try so hard, though with almost as little effect, to address our own children with our adult knowledge, to press our influence on them—or why we engage during our forties and fifties in extended bouts of psychotherapy, attempting to grasp what our child selves may have missed. However much of a simulacrum they may be, such strategies are our way of feeling that we are reaching back and affecting our own pasts. The wish to make that one-way message into a two-way connection is overwhelming.

In *The Child in Time* Ian McEwan briefly grants that wish —for Stephen and, by proxy, for us. It is not, though, to his childhood self that Stephen speaks; in fact, he doesn't even *speak* at all. But he has an experience (a dream? a hallucination? a ghostly encounter?) that briefly carries him back to a scene between two young people in a pub, a man and a woman engaged in animated conversation. Stephen stands outside the pub watching them through a window, so that if they looked up, he imagines, "they might have seen a phantom beyond the spotted glass, immobile with the tension of inarticulated recognition." And then one of them does look up, and for Stephen suddenly "everything was changed . . . He was looking into the eyes of the woman, and he knew who she was . . . Absurdly, he raised his hand and made an awkward gesture, something between a wave and a salute. There was no response from the young woman whom he knew, beyond question, was his mother."

Much later in the novel, the middle-aged Stephen leads his ailing mother into a discussion of her past and, without prompting her with his own experience, gets her to talk about that moment in the pub. She and his father had apparently been discussing whether or not to get married; she was pregnant, but they had almost decided not to have the child. And then she saw a face at the window, "the face of a child, sort of floating there . . . ," she tells Stephen. "It was looking right at me. Thinking about it over the years, I realize it was probably the landlord's boy, or some kid off one of the local farms. But as far as I was concerned then, I was convinced, I just *knew* that I was looking at my own child. If you like, I was looking at you."

In general I do not care for ghost stories, at least in their literary form (though I am a total sucker for all the movies in this genre, from *Truly, Madly, Deeply* to *The Sixth Sense*). But something about Ian McEwan's description of this occasion is so skillful—so cinematic, perhaps—that it captured my imagination on the spot. It is a moment that transcends all the practical questions: about the reality of time-travel, about abortion politics, about the uses of sentiment and sentimentality. It is a moment, if you will, of pure wish-fulfillment.

Recently I asked McEwan if he had ever used anything from a dream in his fiction. "Once," he answered. "It was a dream in which I came out of a forest onto a road, and I knew that if I went round the curve in the road there would be a pub, and that something very important to me would happen there, or had happened there . . . So I put that into one of my novels."

"*The Child in Time*," I said quietly.

"Yes," he said, not seeming surprised at all that I had remembered. Perhaps he thought I had just reread the book. But in fact I was only about to reread it; at that point, I hadn't opened its pages for more than eight years. It was simply that *his* dream, through its transformation in the novel, had become *my* dream, permanently lodged in the part of my memory that I keep for significant things that have happened to me.

THE STRANGE CASE OF
HUCK AND JIM

◢◣◢◣

I CAN REMEMBER almost
nothing about the circumstances surrounding my first reading of *Huckleberry Finn.* This in itself is strange. I know I read
the whole book through once as a teenager, and once again
as a graduate student, but beyond that I draw a blank. I
search my memory in vain for the likely background: my
childhood room at home in Palo Alto, my first Berkeley
apartment, one of the cafés I frequented in my graduate
school days. I can remember these locations on their own,
but none of them feels connected to this novel. It is as if my
first and second encounters with Mark Twain's masterpiece
took place in a void, as if I had entered into a kind of no-
time, no-space reading dislocated from the geography and
chronology of my daily life.

And yet (or perhaps I should say, and so) the novel itself
is virtually all there in my memory, clearer and more specific
than just about any other book. With the other works I've
been rereading lately, the general outline may persist, filled

in on occasion with a few salient details or memorable phrases; I may remember certain characters very well while nearly forgetting others of almost equal importance. But with *Huckleberry Finn* I seem to remember everything. From the opening two authorial notes, both of which strike me as utterly familiar, to the last two sentences of the book—but who does *not* remember Huck preparing to "light out for the Territory"?—I feel as if each sentence, each word, turns out to be just what I was expecting. It almost seems as if I had been born with this novel in my brain, so that even the first reading was merely a reinforcement of what I already knew, and hence unmemorable, lacking the usual primal-scene intensity of a first reading.

This is not to say that the book has not changed for me. Quite the opposite. Because I can remember it so well on a verbal level, I am more than usually aware of the presence of two different readers in me. There is the younger, original reader, who recognizes all the bits of language as they come flying by (so much so that certain words and phrases, like "dasn't" and "skiff" and "swap places" and "spread himself," are associated entirely with this book, having entered my life when I first read it and having remained almost untouched in my mind ever since). And then there is the older reader, who now has more of a context into which to fit all the recognizable bits, as well as more of a desire to do so. That the novel is *about* doubleness—about two selves contained in a single character and two characters who make up a single self; about a whole society or religion or nation that says one thing and means another, and about individuals who do the same; about pretending, or lying, or playacting, or fiction-making, or whatever you want to call it that Huck is so good at—makes this doubleness in my response all the more apparent to me. As with *Don Quixote*, I understood everything important about the book the first time I read it, and yet I understand it much better now. I could feel the complications even as a child, but it is only as a middle-aged adult that I can observe and analyze and make logical sense of them. Still, logical sense takes me only so far; with this book, in particular, a great deal must be left to feeling.

"As with *Don Quixote*" is no idle phrase. Fresh from a rereading of that earlier mold-breaking work, I can see exactly how much Mark Twain meant his novel to be another in that tradition—a tradition consisting, precisely, of only these two books. What a terrifying degree of ambition he must have had, and how amazing that he managed to live up to it. For *Huckleberry Finn* is, indeed, an American *Don Quixote*, with all the complicated layers and self-reflective game-playing and searing intimacy of its Spanish predecessor. Twain's method naturally had to be very different from Cervantes' to accomplish this: slavish imitation would have got him nowhere. (Slavish *anything*, as Twain's novel suggests, only leads us farther downriver, away from the freedom and independence we aim for in a novel.) But the inheritance is still visibly there, from the very first moments of *Huckleberry Finn*.

Cervantes' age was a more leisurely one, so his book could open with a dozen or so pages of prefatory material. Twain, with his eye on the clock, has pared these down to two brief notes. But they are still distinctively quixotic in tone. If the censors of seventeenth-century Spain are bent on threatening us with warnings about the wholesomeness of what we are about to read, Twain's "Notice" from "G. G., Chief of Ordnance" maintains an equally authoritarian voice: "Persons attempting to find a motive in this narrative will be prosecuted; persons attempting to find a moral in it will be banished; persons attempting to find a plot in it will be shot." (This is what I mean by memorable language. Confess that you, too, recognized this sentence, even if you've only read *Huckleberry Finn* once.) Stylistically and tonally, this Notice is all over the map: jocularly folksy and highly polished, officious and rebellious, funny because false, even funnier in a different way because true. "Persons" and "prosecuted" come from the generic, invasive, familiar language of the American legal system, but "banished" comes from somewhere else entirely—Sir Walter Scott, maybe, or Alexandre Dumas. And the word "shot," highlighted by its final placement as well as by the short, sharp crack of its rhyme with "plot," comes straight out of the realm of this novel, a frontier-violence world that is also a Punch-and-Judy show, where death is both comic and shocking, where lynchings, manhunts, and tar-and-featherings are routine entertainments, and where being forcibly "sivilized" is the thing to be most feared and evaded.

If Twain's opening Notice floats somewhere above the plane of literal meaning, the "Explanatory" that follows it is positively stratospheric. Signed simply "The Author," it purports to give us an explanation of the various regional, class, and racial dialects that appear in the book. The stunner comes in the final, stand-alone sentence: "I make this explanation for the reason that without it many readers would suppose that all these characters were trying to talk alike and not succeeding." Everything about Twain's relationship to his audience is contained in miniature here, and the validity of his actual faith in his readers (as opposed to his pretend lack of faith) is proven by the fact that I don't need to explain the joke to anybody. Which is lucky, because the paradox rendered by this sentence is so apparent and yet so delicate that it would collapse under a too-close scrutiny. Still, some glimmer of a profound idea survives our instant penetration of the humor, so that the passage induces in us the same sense of vertigo that Borges derived from *Don Quixote*. Under what circumstances could we possibly suppose that fictional characters were trying but not succeeding at being —what? Some simulacrum or posed version of themselves? Something entirely other than themselves? This is to imag-

ine fictional characters as if they were actors in a play; this is
to equate them with other kinds of living creatures who are
at least as real as their Author. (A skeptic about religion, as
Twain was and as I am, might even say *more* real.) Nor is this
a preposterous notion. In a very visceral way, Don Quixote
and Sancho Panza, Huck and Jim are now more alive for us
than either Cervantes or Twain.

Cervantes' creatures, at any rate, are very much alive for
Mark Twain, and Don Quixote is an explicit presence in
Huckleberry Finn. Twain is fascinated by the readerly mirror
effect—an imagined character who has read too many fictional accounts of knighthood, and who therefore takes on
the role of an imaginary knight—and he loops the loop by
having *his* fictional characters imitate that knight. Tom
Sawyer is, as usual in such cases, the instigator. Near the beginning of the novel, when Huck is still living with the
Widow Dawson, Tom has his gang of boys swear a complicated and bloody oath of allegiance. "Everybody said it was
a real beautiful oath," Huck tells us, "and asked Tom if he
got it out of his own head. He said some of it, but the rest
was out of pirate-books and robber-books and every gang
that was high-toned had it." If we are thinking about
Cervantes at all, we will be put on the alert here, so it will
come as no surprise (well, only a very *little* surprise) when, a
few pages later, Huck challenges some of Tom's wilder
imaginings.

> I didn't see no di'monds, and I told Tom Sawyer so. He said
> there was loads of them there, anyway, and he said there
> was A-rabs there, too, and elephants and things. I said, why
> couldn't we see them then? He said if I warn't so ignorant but
> had read a book called *Don Quixote,* I would know without
> asking. He said it was all done by enchantment.

The question of exactly who is ignorant, and what counts
as ignorance, and which kinds of ignorance are the most

damning, will recur often in this novel. Tom always plays the know-it-all role with Huck, and Huck sometimes plays it with Jim, and in pretty much every case Twain gets us to back the ignoramus. Book-learning and book-imitating are both suspect, so that Tom's eventual insistence on doing Jim's prison break "by the book" comes to seem the worst kind of ignorance of all. Yet this is not just a matter of glorifying the innocent Rousseauian savage (though many readers have seen Jim as exactly that: an exemplar of uncivilized virtue). Twain is too canny to take that sentimental line. He plays with ignorance and knowledge as if they were differently weighted juggling balls, and sometimes he has so many balls in the air at once that he can't fully keep track of them. Huck himself, for instance, veers wildly from a boy who can't spell a simple name like George Jackson to an accomplished biblical scholar capable of arguing up a logical storm. Even his way of speaking alters with the situation, so that Huck finally comes off as the ultimate character who is "trying to talk alike and not succeeding." And our own knowledge appears to be a variable quality as well. At times we are expected to recognize literary references, understand historical or dramatic parodies, and even deplore the tastelessness of an overdecorated middle-class parlor; at times we are supposed to despise all such knowledge as useless intellectual hogwash. Being a fool is hardly desirable, but being fooled is one of the great pleasures of the novel, particularly this novel. *Huckleberry Finn* repeatedly, and in the end relentlessly, asks us to consider exactly how much fooling we can tolerate.

The end of the novel—by which I mean the whole last quarter or more—has always been a problem, for me and for everyone else. No one can bear that long sequence when Jim is locked up as a runaway slave and Tom endlessly delays his release by making an elaborate game of it. I thought a lot about this problem before I started out this time, and it worried me, so I kept my eyes peeled for any advance notice that the ending had been adequately prepared for. And such signs are plentiful, if you look for them. From the opening pages, you can see Tom fooling Jim just for the pleasure of the joke, and later you can see Huck doing the same thing during the crucial fog scene, when he tries to persuade Jim that they were never really lost and separated. (I will come back to this scene in a moment.) And Jim is not the only victim of the game, though his victimization is certainly the most poignant. All through the novel we see Huck fooling people—not just for self-preservation, the way Jim does, and not just for money, the way the fake Duke and Dauphin do, and not even out of religious or social hypocrisy, the way so many of the minor characters do. No, Huck fools people just for the fun of it, because he enjoys making things up. Why else would he become a different character with a different name every time he hits a new town? It would be a lot simpler and more effective just to use the same name every time; in that case he wouldn't risk forgetting his new name, which is a recurrent problem. But Huck doesn't just make things up because *he* enjoys it. He also does it because *we* enjoy it. The lies he tells are the fuel that keeps the novel going, augmented by the equally amusing lies of other characters we meet along the way. There we are, running along in high gear, getting a real kick out of all this fooling, when suddenly—wham!—Mark Twain hits us in the face with that ending. And no matter how justified the ending may be by all the advance notice Twain has given us, it is still a terrible annoyance to plow through it. There is no way around the discomfort of that horribly drawn-out conclusion.

When I was younger, I had a theory about the ending that I thought might salvage it. You could call it the Theory of the False Bottom. The idea was that Mark Twain loved his characters so much he couldn't bear to part with them, and he imagined that we'd have trouble saying goodbye to them too. So, out of the softness of his heart, he constructed a sort of magician's escape hatch, a big, fat, fake ending that didn't really end the novel. It was just a front, a setup, behind which the characters, like Houdini, could invisibly slip away. So *Huckleberry Finn* never really had to end, because the real ending was permanently hidden from us.

Like all theories, or at least all *my* theories, this one doesn't hold up so well in the face of experience. If my theory were correct, the experience of finishing *Huckleberry Finn* would be one of wistful, gentle incompletion. Instead, it is an experience of tremendous, ever-mounting irritation. Mark Twain has poured a great deal of anger into this ending—the very opposite of the kindly softheartedness I once envisioned—and we readers are soaking it up like a sponge. We want to *kill* Tom Sawyer, just plain get *rid* of him, and we want to get Jim out of that stupid, embarrassing situation with all the snakes and rats and rope ladders and female disguises and blood-scrawled messages on plates that Tom (with Huck's somewhat unwilling connivance) has introduced to make this escape as much as possible like a scene from *The Count of Monte Cristo.* And the curious thing is, we want this whether or not we know how the novel ends. If we've read the book before, we know that Jim has already been set free by Miss Watson's will, so the delay seems gratuitously cruel. But if we don't know that—and Mark Twain very carefully doesn't let Huck *or* us in on that secret until the end—the delay is agonizing in a different way: we think that Jim's freedom is actually at stake, and that these stupid games are dangerously, idiotically jeopardizing it. But even *that* is authorially counterproductive, because the joke, by anyone's standards, goes on way too long, so that no shred of suspense could possibly survive. Twain, in the guise of Tom, just won't let up on us, and by the end all we want is for him to quit fooling around.

This is the man, remember, whose sense of timing is so perfect that he can make you laugh out loud in the solitude of your own living room. This is the author who, like his model Cervantes, can anticipate your response more than a century before you make it. Do we really think he could write a woefully tedious ending by mistake?

This time through, I was acutely aware of how many moments in *Huckleberry Finn* culminate in a feeling of discomfort—how much the book as a whole is built on that feeling. Discomfort and humor: those are the twin pillars that support this novel, and, as one might expect from Twain, they are Siamese twins, joined at the hip. Among the funniest parts of *Huckleberry Finn* are its jokes about death. There are dead-baby jokes, coldblooded-killer jokes, people-returned-from-the-dead jokes, people-expecting-to-die jokes ("we et up the sawdust and it gave us a most amazing stomache-ache. We reckoned we was all going to die, but didn't"). The entire section about the artworks left by Emmeline Granger-ford—those hilariously sentimental pictures which I remembered caption for caption and image for image from my last reading more than twenty years ago—would not be nearly so funny if Emmeline had not died young. And this kind of humor is sprinkled through a book in which the amount of *actual* violence and killing is, to an adult reader, somewhat shocking. (It was not shocking to me as a teen-ager, just as it is not shocking to Huck, who is about the age I was when I first read the book.) Like all black-humorists—or, for that matter, all slapstick comedians—Twain is adept at using the combination of humor and violence. Nor is he trapped in the humorous mode. He can turn on a dime from mockery to pathos, as he does, for instance, with the Grangerfords, when they all die in the bloody feud with the Shepherdsons and Huck is left to cover the body of the boy who befriended him.

But none of this is what I mean by discomfort. After all, we are reasonably accustomed to the shock element we find in Twain's comedy; it's the basis of most humor, not just *Huckleberry Finn's*. The kind of discomfort that distinguishes this novel from other humorous books is the kind you actually *feel* as discomfort. It's not funny, and it's not enjoyable. And though it's necessarily a sense of moral rather than physical discomfort, it comes through so powerfully that it can almost make you wriggle in your seat. The sense of discomfort *Huckleberry Finn* excels at producing is closely allied to a feeling of shame.

Let me go back now to that scene on the raft in the fog, that important moment when (as we later find out) Huck and Jim unwittingly drift past the Cairo landing, the turnoff to their planned northward journey, and thus miss the immediate chance of freedom. You might say this is the moment that sets up the long, convoluted ending, because if he hadn't missed the Cairo juncture, Jim probably wouldn't have needed Tom Sawyer to "free" him. It sets the ending up in other ways, too. Huck, who has been separated from Jim in the fog, sees their reunion as the opportunity to engage in one of his make-believe routines, and he uses all his persuasive talents to convince Jim that the whole fog episode was just a dream. (This should also, by the way, make us recall *Don Quixote*, which has its own was-it-a-dream sequence in the Cave of Montesinos episode. But the trickery that the Don and Sancho practice on each other is always more mutual and less intentional than that perpetrated by Huck on Jim.) He even goes so far as to allow Jim to interpret for him the symbolic meaning of the various elements in the "dream." Jim takes all this very seriously—in part because he has been so worried at losing Huck in the fog, and so relieved to find him alive—so it is a tremendous shock to him when Huck finally shows his comedic hand, just as the day is beginning to clear:

> "Oh, well, that's all interpreted well enough as far as it goes, Jim," I says, "but what does *these* things stand for?"

It was the leaves and rubbish on the raft and the smashed oar. You could see them first-rate now.

Confronted with this evidence of the fog's reality and hence of Huck's purposeful lies, Jim is silent for a moment. And then he answers:

> "What do dey stan' for? I's gwyne to tell you. When I got all wore out wid work, en wid de callin' for you, en went to sleep, my heart wuz mos' broke bekase you wuz los', en I didn' k'yer no mo' what become er me en de raf'. En when I wake up en fine you back agin, all safe en soun', de tears come, en I could 'a' got down on my knees en kiss yo' foot, I's so thankful. En all you wuz thinkin' 'bout wuz how you could make a fool uv ole Jim wid a lie. Dat truck dah is *trash*; en trash is what people is dat puts dirt on de head er dey fren's en makes 'em ashamed."

I can no longer remember how I felt when I first read the fog section of the book—whether I enjoyed Huck's game until we got to this final point, or whether it made me uncomfortable from the start. Now I can only see the trickery as the prelude to Jim's devastating speech; I can only view it as an excessively drawn out, not particularly entertaining piece of cruel foolery, like the annoying ending in a reduced form.

The sense of shame is pervasive—not just the shame that Jim says he feels at being tricked, but also the shame we feel on Huck's behalf, a shame which he, to give him credit, feels himself. ("It made me feel so mean I could almost kissed *his* foot to get him to take it back.") And the sense of shame applies to us too, for aren't we the audience Huck was seeking to entertain with this joke? And haven't we been entertained —if not by this, then by other, similar lies? Granted, there is a difference between lying to someone who cares for you, as Jim evidently cares for Huck, and lying to someone who does not necessarily have your interest at heart, which is how Huck could reasonably classify most of the strangers he comes across. But even that is not the deepest source of our discomfort here. More to the point, there is a difference between trying to make a fool out of another white person—if you are white—and trying to make a fool out of a black one. We can't help feeling, in fact, that Huck never would have tried this kind of joke on a white person, because he believes that dreams and superstitions and interpretations of bad-luck signs are all part of the black mentality. (This too comes up again at the end, when Tom and Huck persuade the black sentry guarding Jim that he is not really seeing and hearing the things he thinks he is, because he is the victim of witchcraft. It's not funny there, either, but it's less painful than it is in the case of Huck and Jim, because there's no bond of prior affection with the sentry.)

A great deal of our discomfort, in the fog scene, hinges on our sense of the black/white difference—a difference in power, obviously, rather than just a difference in skin color or cultural beliefs or modes of speech. And Jim's response, affecting as it is, heightens the discomfort by stressing the difference between us readers and Jim. The point is not necessarily that we are white and Jim is black—the novel, though it is addressing us directly, can never be sure who "we" are, and in any case that entity is bound to change over time, and even to fluctuate in the very process of an individual reading, because we respond to fiction as something other than just our physical, historical selves. But part of our identity, as a reading "we," derives from the novel itself, and this novel presumes we are more like Huck than like Jim. Huck may speak in a version of the vernacular, complete with slang and grammatical errors, but he is essentially speaking our language, whereas Jim's dialect is drastically distorted, purposely alienating—even, or especially, if our skin color is closer to Jim's than to Huck's. Jim's *Amos 'n' Andy* version of black speech is painful to read, and not just for the usual reason that dialect, whether in Dickens or Balzac or Twain, is always painful to read: that is, because it makes the written language almost incomprehensible. In this instance, the pain of indecipherability has been given an extra moral punch by being linked to the pain of humiliation. No wonder they don't teach this novel in high schools. It would be paralyzingly embarrassing for anyone, teacher or student, to read aloud a passage like Jim's speech in a mixed-race classroom. And that embarrassment is not something that has randomly or coincidentally accrued to the language in the hundred and twenty years since Twain set it down. He put the embarrassment in there, deliberately. He meant us to feel ashamed.

If you need evidence for this, you need look no further than the second paragraph after Jim's speech, the one that follows Huck's statement about how mean he felt. "It was fifteen minutes before I could work myself up to go and humble myself to a nigger—but I done it and I warn't sorry for it afterward, either," Huck assures us. There are other passages in the book where we see him wrestling in a similar way with his conscience—about whether it's wrong to be robbing Miss Watson of her human property, for instance, or about whether Jim is evil when he talks of stealing his children out of slavery—and in all of them Huck resorts to the word "nigger."

Like the word "idiot" in Dostoyevsky's novel, this word is deployed throughout *Huckleberry Finn* as an intentional weapon, a sharp, pointed object. Even when it is used casually by the townspeople Huck meets on his journey, the casualness is itself part of the effect: these people and the whole culture in which they dwell are obliviously cruel, obliviously vicious. The word "nigger" may have acquired new layers of meaning in the past century or so (the *Random House Historical Dictionary of American Slang* gives it nine closely printed pages, with most of the examples coming from the last fifty years), but its basic intent—to offend or disparage—is still the same as it was in Twain's time. The intensity with which the word is rejected has increased of late (over the last twenty-five years, for instance, the *American Heritage Dictionary of the English Language* has reclassified it from "vulgar" to "offensive slang"), but it was always held at arm's length. "A Southern gentleman rarely, if ever, says *nigger*," announces an 1860 citation from the *Dictionary of American Slang*. Huck Finn, of course, is no gentleman, and part of what Mark Twain does with this narrator is to rip the cover off polite convention. Ladies and gentlemen up and down the Mississippi might not have *used* the word, but they would nonetheless have benefited from the social arrangement that gave rise to it. Twain wants to assault his well-mannered readers with the ugly little secret that underlies their lives; he wants to force them to hear it spoken out loud.

But the social order described in *Huckleberry Finn* has changed by the time Mark Twain is writing the book, and this too is part of the novel's purposeful discomfort. It's all very well to get behind Jim's freedom in 1885, when the book comes out; it's all very well to root for runaway slaves twenty years after they've been set free. Our sympathy doesn't cost us much, in these circumstances. And it's precisely this lack of investment, this terrible discrepancy between the painfulness of the slave experience and our ex post facto ease in deploring it, that Twain uses against us in the last quarter of the novel. He sets it up so all this imaginative energy is being used to free a slave who is, in fact, already free. As Tom Sawyer might say, where's the glory in that? Where's the source of self-congratulation?

Unlike *Uncle Tom's Cabin*, which washes us clean in its saccharine tears, *Huckleberry Finn* doesn't cede us the high moral ground. It leaves us feeling kind of rotten, the way Huck felt after he fooled Jim about the fog. "You want tall-tale entertainment?" Mark Twain seems to be snarling. "You want a funny adventure story based on the escape of a black slave? Okay, I'll give it to you until you're sick of it." And we are, by the end. We blithely took the pleasure he doled out for the first three-quarters of the book and, by god, he makes us pay for it, with *nigger* dinning in our ears ever more frequently as the novel draws to its close.

The strangest thing of all, for me, is that time doesn't dim the unnerving power of this novel. Reconstruction comes and goes, the Ku Klux Klan rises and falls, the armed forces and the public schools get integrated, black athletes and comedians vanquish their white competitors, and the word "nigger" just goes on getting more and more upsetting. If I look at my own life, I see that since first reading the novel I have moved from a lily-white suburb to a much more integrated community; since last reading it, I have married a man raised in Harlem, whose two half-brothers are black. And yet I am still no closer than I ever was to closing the gap this novel portrays and enacts.

Huckleberry Finn, it now seems to me, is not a novel about slave times. If it were, its ability to charm and wound us would pretty much have ceased with its publication. It is, instead, a novel about all of America's most uncrossable barriers, and about our commendable but thus far hopeless desire to cross them. Those idyllic moments on the river represent that desire in its purest form, as a wish fulfilled, but those moments are just a dream. The reality is trash, and dirt, and shame—and laughter, which sometimes brings us together and sometimes (they are often the same times) tears us apart.

A LITERARY CAREER

O<small>N A TRIP</small> to New York, I decide to reread *A Hazard of New Fortunes.*

Everyone who hears what I am reading says, "Oh, how appropriate for New York." Even the people who have not read the Howells novel say this, because they all know about it from a *New Yorker* article written by Adam Gopnik. Gopnik, a literary man who has recently looked for an apartment in New York, is mainly interested in the chapters about a literary man looking for an apartment in New York—a desperate situation which seems to have improved not at all since the late nineteenth century. Scarcity and demand are still the prime New York characteristics, and not just in terms of apartments. I sense it even in regard to William Dean Howells. If Gopnik is bidding on him, can I afford to compete?

This sensation of being moved in on particularly disturbs me because I have been staking a quiet and uncompetitive claim on Howells for the past twenty years or more. Ever since picking up *The Story of a Play* in a dilapidated old copy, I have been collecting and reading him. He has been hard to get, being mostly out of print, but I have worked hard to accumulate his volumes, and I especially treasure the editions printed by J. A. Howells & Co., the family firm back in Ohio. Over the years I have come to view my passion as virtuously unpossessive—at times I even urge others to write about him, having no wish to do so myself—but then, when I see him there in the pages of *The New Yorker,* I feel robbed.

I date my personal feeling for Howells back to about 1980, but my acquaintance with him started even earlier, when I first read *Hazard* and its more famous companion, *The Rise of Silas Lapham,* as an undergraduate. Apparently I didn't think much about them one way or the other. "He isn't Henry James" is probably how I would have put it, and let it go at that, as if there were only one desirable way to be a novelist. Henry James himself knew better. In a letter written May 17, 1890, James told his friend Howells that

> the *Hazard* is simply prodigious . . . you have never yet done anything so roundly & totally good . . . In fact your reservoir deluges me, altogether, with surprise as well as other sorts of effusion: by which I mean that though you do much to empty it you keep it remarkably full. I seem to myself, in comparison, to fill mine with a teaspoon & obtain but a trickle. However, I don't mean to compare myself with you or to compare you, in the particular case, with anything but life . . . The novelist is a particular *window,* absolutely, & of worth in so far as he is one; and it's because you open so well & are hung so close over the street that *I* could hang out of it all day long.

That window makes me think of Howells's beloved Italy, where he served as American consul and wrote his first novels (and where, more than a century later, I basked in the bath of a Venice hotel room, reading those early works in the Library of America edition). It also reminds me of the North

End in Boston, the city where, as a college student, I first encountered Howells. It was here that he established himself as a major literary force, the so-to-speak "dean" of American letters, an editor and writer and friend of other writers (including, people always like to point out, Mark Twain *and* Henry James, as if no one else could sincerely value both). And it evokes as well the New York in which, for a time, Howells pursued his literary career, much in the manner of his character Basil March, who in *A Hazard of New Fortunes* moves from Boston to New York to take up the editorship of a new magazine. Prodigious vitality—the same quality James admires in Howells's writing—is what strikes March about the street life of his new city, particularly in the poorer neighborhoods, where he observes how the "fire escapes, with their light iron balconies and ladders of iron, decorated the lofty house fronts; the roadway and sidewalks and doorsteps swarmed with children; women's heads seemed to show at every window."

Rereading this novel in New York, I am particularly struck by how the city has and has not changed since Howells's time. I never saw the Third Avenue El, which Basil March calls "the most beautiful thing in New York—the one always and certainly beautiful thing here," and which Mrs. March views as "the most ideal way of getting about in the world"; it had disappeared by the time I first visited the city. Nor does the Lower East Side resemble the neighborhood Howells describes. At this exact moment (the kind of moment that passes so quickly in New York), it's a formerly dullish area just starting to get youthfully hip: an incipient SoHo, an up-and-coming TriBeCa. But in 1890 it vibrated with a mixture of newly arrived life, including even a "Dickensy, cockneyish . . . shabby-genteel ballad-seller" of whom March asked directions when he found himself lost in that "frantic panorama." All this has altered beyond recognition.

But the Greenwich Village of the late nineteenth century

is still perceptibly there, with its "streets of small brick houses, with here and there one painted red, and the mortar lines picked out in white, and with now and then a fine wooden portal of fluted pillars and a bowed transom . . . and the new apartment houses, breaking the old skyline with their towering stories." March and his wife liked to sit "in the softening evenings among the infants and dotards of Latin extraction in Washington Square, safe from all who knew them"—which, minus the unfortunate ethnic remark, is just what you can do today. Farther uptown, you can still see streets "which had been mostly built up in apartment houses, with here and there a single dwelling dropped far down beneath and beside them, to that jagged-toothed effect on the skyline so often observable in such New York streets." Above all, the city retains its sense of distinction from all other cities in the world, with "the sort of people whom you would know for New Yorkers elsewhere, so well appointed and so perfectly kept at all points," and the neighborhoods to which "New York gave its peculiar stamp," so that visitors might "find One-hundred-and-twenty-fifth Street inchoately like Twenty-third Street and Fourteenth Street," despite their obvious differences.

March's offices—the home of *Every Other Week,* a fortnightly magazine—are located in a converted townhouse on West Eleventh Street. I, during this visit, am staying with a friend in a townhouse on West Twelfth Street. Basil March has come to New York to begin his literary career, and I have come to celebrate mine, for the real occasion of my trip is a twentieth-anniversary party for the quarterly magazine I edit. It is therefore easy for me to project my life into March's world and his into mine: he might almost be one of the guests flocking to the Victorian robber baron's mansion (now a private club) where my party is taking place. Twenty years may feel like a long time to me, but a hundred and ten seems almost nothing.

Perhaps it is a mistake to be reading this book at precisely this point in my life. The description of the city itself is so enticing as to make me nearly weep. Why, I ask myself, did I fail to come to New York to seek my fortune straight after leaving Boston? Where was the Fulkerson who might have offered me such an editorship, the Dryfoos who could have paid for the magnificent start-up? Had I missed a terrific opportunity in exiling myself to my native California? Who would I be now if I had come here instead? For days I brood on these questions, finding myself in the unenviable position of envying a fictional character.

Of course, I could still move to New York. I may be middle-aged, but then so was Basil March. In fact, I am shocked on rereading the book to see the extent to which it is about middle age; no wonder it had so little impact on me at twenty. It is Basil's age which makes the hazard of his undertaking so great. "What a noble thing life is anyway!" he remarks toward the end of the novel. "Here I am, well on the way to fifty, after twenty-five years of hard work, looking forward to the potential poorhouse as confidently as I did in youth." Back in Boston, he at least had a settled life, a comfortable family existence, a house that he and his wife loved. At twenty, or even thirty, I could not have understood what it meant to say about a house, "They had beautified it in every way and had unconsciously taken credit to themselves for it. They felt, with a glow almost of virtue, how perfectly it fitted their lives and their children's, and they believed that somehow it expressed their characters—that it was like them." As an undergraduate, I could only have heard Howells's note of mockery here; now I can also hear the note of truth.

Henry James didn't much care for the novel's title ("I confess I shld. have liked to change the name for you"), but I don't see how it could be bettered. Every word is doing double duty. A "hazard" is a danger, but also a reasonable risk or gamble, as in "hazarding a guess." If you never hazard anything, you run another kind of risk, that of premature stasis; and if you aren't willing to risk even your new fortunes once you've got them, you may become as imprisoned in them as you were in your old life. Whether or not "new" is a good thing is precisely what's being debated throughout much of the book: a new job, a new home, new agglomerations of wealth, new relations between capital and labor. As for "fortunes," they are at once the potential riches of the metropolis —that eternal New York theme—and the turns of fate, the results of good luck and bad, the twists a life can take unexpectedly.

My own unexpected twist comes on the third day of my New York trip, when I am about fifty pages into the Howells novel. Already my envy of March's new fortunes is in full swing. I feel almost willing to hazard anything, even my beloved Berkeley house, in order to live in New York. But nothing so extreme, it turns out, will be required of me. My deus ex machina, my Fulkerson-backed-by-Dryfoos, comes in the form of a phone call from the Columbia Journalism School, informing me that I have won a fellowship. I am invited to come to Manhattan, all expenses paid, for three months the next year.

Of course there is the family situation to be negotiated. "I don't approve of it," says Basil's wife, Isabel, when he tells her of the possible move to New York. She cites the children's schooling, her own attachments to Boston. Basil agrees, but nonetheless feels resentful. "He knew that she had really tried to consent to a thing that was repugnant to her, and in his heart he gave her more credit for the effort than he had allowed her openly. She knew that she had made it with the reservation he accused her of, and that he had a right to feel sore at what she could not help. But he left her to brood over his ingratitude, and she suffered him to go heavy and unfriended to meet the chances of the day."

A Hazard of New Fortunes is, among other things, a telling portrait of a long-term marriage. Howells is astute about the constant small negotiations that need to take place between two bound-together personalities, the unspoken battles and truces, the ever-mounting pile of things that have been swept under the carpet. "She expected him in this event to do as he pleased, and she resigned herself to it with considerable comfort in holding him accountable. He learned to expect this, and after suffering keenly from her disappointment with whatever he did, he waited patiently till she forgot her grievance and began to extract what consolation lurks in the irreparable. She would almost admit at moments that what he had done was a very good thing, but she reserved the right to return in full force to her original condemnation of it; and she accumulated each act of independent volition in witness and warning against him."

With the sexes reversed, this is a remarkably accurate portrayal of my negotiations with my husband over the New York fellowship. He does not want me to go to New York while his job keeps him stuck in California. He reminds me that I have a child in school; I point out that the child, at fifteen, is practically self-supervising. I say something about the importance of this opportunity to my literary career. ("Basil," she appealed solemnly, "have I ever interfered with your career?") My husband, however, is no Isabel March: when I say "literary career," he hears "cocktail parties." I try another tack, and still another, all this taking place by long-distance phone, late at night, while I am staying in other people's houses—not the ideal circumstances for marital discussion. We can each feel the usual dynamic operating: my powerful will, his equally powerful resistance to it. ("He owned this defect of temperament, but he said that it compensated for the opposite in her character. 'I suppose that's one of the chief uses of marriage; people supplement each other and form a pretty fair sort of human being together.

The only drawback to the theory is that unmarried people seem each as complete and whole as a married pair.'") At last we arrive at a compromise: I will go to New York for two months rather than three, and I will take our son with me for part of the time.

In the meantime, as is always the case, the process of winning the battle has slightly cheapened the prize for me. Is it *really* that great to live in New York? Daily life, even on a one-week trip, suggests otherwise. (In the ladies' room at Columbia, preparing to meet my newly acquired patrons, I scan the mirror and notice that my skin has already begun to break out. "A New York day is very hard on the face," I comment to the woman standing at the sink next to mine. She answers dryly, "That's one way of putting it.") And I go back to the Howells book almost a little fearfully: what other new fortunes, or other revelations about my old fortunes, lie in store for me in its pages?

I don't mean to suggest that I am rereading the novel merely as a kind of fantastically prophetic handbook for editors. Basil March may share his author's profession, but there is very little in *A Hazard of New Fortunes* about the job of editing itself. Still, what there is could only have been written by a practiced professional. We learn, for instance, that March feels able to admire the first issue of *Every Other Week* "because he had not only not written it, but in a way had not edited it. To be sure, he had chosen all the material, but he had not voluntarily put it together for that number; it had largely put itself together, as every number of every magazine does and as it seems more and more to do in the experience of every editor." Reading this, I am pleased to discover how closely my miniaturized experience on *The Threepenny Review* echoes Howells's much grander experience at *Harper's*. Nor, despite my isolation in California, do I seem to be missing out on a lot of collegial hobnobbing. "Most of the contributors came from a distance," Howells says of March's New York job; "even the articles written in

New York reached him through the post, and so far from having his valuable time, as they called it, consumed in interviews with his collaborators, he rarely saw any of them." And if we hear little of the collaborators, we hear even less of their collaborations. In fact, Howells's novel doesn't give us much feeling at all for what *Every Other Week* is actually like, as a written object intended to be read. But then, most tales of literary magazines—from Margaret Anderson's *My Thirty Years' War,* her autobiographical account of *The Little Review,* to George Gissing's fictional *New Grub Street*—focus less on literary content than they do on the business of keeping the magazine (or the magazine writer) alive.

The business of publishing—the question of who owns the magazine, and how that power is exercised—is certainly at the heart of *A Hazard of New Fortunes.* At first the subject is introduced jokingly. "It gave March a disagreeable feeling of being owned and of being about to be inspected by his proprietor," Howells tells us, as Dryfoos is about to visit the premises for the first time. We can tell by the word "proprietor" (more appropriate to a shop or a restaurant) that March doesn't *really* feel a magazine can be "owned" in that way. But later the joke becomes all too real when Dryfoos tells March he has to fire a particular employee, an old German radical whose privately held opinions, though never expressed in the magazine, are nonetheless offensive to its owner. Fulkerson, the publisher, sees no problem with this demand, but March invokes the principle of editorial independence.

> "Why, of course, March," said Fulkerson coaxingly, "I mean to do the right thing. But Dryfoos owns the magazine—"
>
> "He doesn't own *me,*" said March, rising. "He has made the little mistake of speaking to me as if he did."

And March courageously offers to resign rather than carry out Dryfoos's wishes against his own better judgment.

Luckily for March, Howells gets him out of this little mess

by having Dryfoos capitulate on the immediate issue, and eventually March and Fulkerson are able to buy the magazine from Dryfoos on quite favorable terms, since the old millionaire is moving his family to Europe after the sudden death of his only son. But such plot resolutions do little to assuage the anxieties raised in the course of the novel. Once you notice that it matters who owns the means of production —even, or especially, the production of words—it becomes difficult to forget this knowledge under cover of a temporary happy ending. And I wonder, in any case, how much Howells wants us to forget it.

There is a great deal in *A Hazard of New Fortunes* about the ownership of labor. It extends far beyond the specific case of *Every Other Week*, ranging from the crackpot theories of an old Southern gentleman who wants to return to the days of slavery, to the strike on the El that finishes up the book (by finishing up Dryfoos Junior, a guileless martyr who is killed by random gunfire when he attempts to intervene in the strike). It's hard to say exactly where the narrative voice comes out, politically. Basil March, certainly, is not fully sympathetic with the strikers, and he explicitly disowns the radical ideas of his employee Lindau even while defending Lindau's right to hold them. But then, March is not necessarily his author's mouthpiece; at one point, indeed, Howells tells us that Basil "had always been too self-enwrapt to perceive the chaos to which the individual selfishness must always lead," and that even his formless apprehension of this truth, as he saw it displayed on the streets of New York, was "nothing definite, nothing better than a vague discomfort." The novel, finally, shows itself to be even braver than its main character in its willingness to bring up uncomfortable subjects and put forth unpopular ideas. In those boom times that came a quarter-century after the Civil War (just as our own boom times came twenty-five years after Vietnam), it could not have been easy or simple for William Dean Howells to question the terms of the new, rich America. He had, after all, reaped its benefits.

It is only now, on finishing *A Hazard of New Fortunes* for a second time, that I begin to realize the extent to which my initial reading of the Howells novel may have affected me. It's not, of course, as if I read the book at twenty and said, "Well, that's that. No commercial magazine career for *me*, thank you, if those are the moral compromises entailed." I barely knew what moral compromises were, at that age—or rather, I didn't know how cunningly they lie in wait for us around each of life's turning points. But some time after first reading *A Hazard of New Fortunes*, I gave up a place in law school to go read literature in England, joined the British Labour Party while I was over there, and then founded my own little nonprofit magazine after I got back to California. How much this series of events can be traced to Howells's direct influence, and how much to the spirit of the age, is a moot point. The fact is that I already knew, when I started *The Threepenny Review* in 1980, something I seemed to have forgotten twenty years later when I began to reread *A Hazard of New Fortunes:* that a rich backer and an editorially independent career are almost by definition mutually exclusive. What I found myself belatedly longing for on my recent New York trip—a wealthy Manhattan publisher's protective embrace—was something I had once, with good reason, consciously evaded. Rereading the Howells novel has reminded me of the ways in which I was right the first time.

It comes time, eventually, for me to leave New York. I have finished *A Hazard of New Fortunes* and therefore need something new to read on the flight home, so, just before going to the airport, I stop in at the newsstand on the corner of West Twelfth and Hudson to buy the latest issue of *The New Yorker*. To my dismay, I see that it is the Money issue—possibly the worst of the magazine's newly invented annual theme issues, and certainly the one that always makes me least eager to live in the city. "Oh, well," I think, "this will make me glad to leave Manhattan." And then, as I stand on line to buy the magazine, the man standing in back of me begins joking with the proprietor behind the counter. Both are immigrants from India, to judge by the sound of their voices and the look of their faces, and both are just as obviously true New Yorkers.

"Well, I just dropped in to say hello," says the one behind me.

"Oh, right, *sure* you did. We never see you anymore. For weeks you never come in here. Now that there's no business to be done with us, you forget all about us. We're no good to you anymore—"

"Oh, yes, it's all about money. Especially in New York, nothing but money." And they both laugh hilariously.

I realize, looking at these two guys, that this is the New York William Dean Howells loved: immigrant New York, lively New York, smart, skeptical, working New York. The El may be down, but some things never change. Manhattan reinvents itself generation after generation, from a million new gene pools, but always in its own image. And thinking about all this, watching those guys laugh (their laughter includes pleasure at their own friendship, but also a sardonic awareness of how much money *does* matter here), I realize I will be very sorry to leave the city after all.

HITCHCOCK'S <u>VERTIGO</u>

Movies are, of course, a different case. One doesn't reread them in precisely the way one does a book. But they can be seen and seen again over the years, at intervals which allow the same kinds of transformations and rediscoveries that books produce when reread over time. And certain movies—in particular, for me, this one—lend themselves to my subject in a way that is finally irresistible.

In 1958, when *Vertigo* first came out, movies were not quite the willed, eternally accessible experience they are today. You couldn't just pop down to your local video rental place or order up the film online. You had to wait for the movie to appear in its own good time, first in a theater in your neighborhood and then, at unpredictable intervals, on TV. Sometimes it would come back to the theaters as a revival, but that too was unpredictable—especially so in the case of *Vertigo*, which for complicated movie-industry reasons was actually taken off the market for over fifteen years.

If you saw *Vertigo* at all during that blacked-out period, it was likely to be in a bootleg or film-archive version, not in a commercial theater, and certainly not on television.

I wasn't taken to *Vertigo* the year it came out—I was only six, after all—but I know I saw it within a few years after that, by the time I was ten, say. In those days we went to Alfred Hitchcock's movies for much the same reasons we watched his television show episodes, because they were entertaining and scary and witty and featured brief, amusing appearances by the director himself. We didn't know we were watching art; we were just having fun. (This was true of the children, naturally, but I think it was also true of the adults. For art, they watched Kurosawa and Bergman and Godard, not Hitchcock.)

I have very clear but incomplete memories of that first viewing, and they are mostly visual memories. I also have a very strong emotional recollection of Bernard Herrmann's haunting music, though, since I am terrible at remembering the details of musical phrases, this is the kind of memory that I only recognized as a memory when I heard the music again. I know that at the age of ten I was particularly struck by the scenes set at Mission San Juan Batista, which was located about sixty miles south of my house and which I had recently visited with my fifth-grade class as part of our California Missions curriculum. I also remember finding the love story hokey and embarrassing, in the way that pre-adolescents do; the extended kiss between Jimmy Stewart and Kim Novak, with its now-famous 360-degree camera angle and its surging musical theme, seemed to me especially ridiculous.

A decade and a half went by before I saw the movie again. This time I was in my mid-twenties, a graduate student at Berkeley, and Ed Snow—the same Edward Snow in whose seminar I had first read *Paradise Lost,* a year or so earlier—was showing *Vertigo* to a film class of his. I was not taking the class, but since the movie was at that time very difficult to see (it was during the blackout period), Ed invited friends and former students to fill up the empty seats during the unpublicized daytime showing at Pacific Film Archive. I can still, nearly twenty-five years later, recall in detail the powerful impact of that second viewing. I wasn't expecting it, since my response the first time had been mainly cerebral, but this time I was swept away by feeling. I am tempted to say, "It was as if I had never seen the movie before," but that is exactly *not* what it was: I was aware, even at the time, that what I was getting was the benefit of a second viewing. The first time I was too caught up in the suspense, and if that is your primary motive, the end of *Vertigo* can be a bit disappointing. But once you know how it ends, you are freed to focus on the emotional progression of the film. For the first time I saw how much the movie was about loss, and about second chances — both subjects that I newly and deeply cared about, at the age of twenty-four. What had seemed melodramatic and hokey to me before now seemed tragic and true: *this* was what love was like, I thought, and nothing other than Shakespeare's *Antony and Cleopatra* had shown it to me so clearly.

And what was it I thought I was learning about love from *Vertigo?* (No, that condescending tone is unfair: I *was* learning, or at the very least confirming what I had begun to suspect.) Well, all the usual things that people who have ever had their hearts even mildly broken — almost all of us, that is — have taken from this movie over the years. That you temporarily lose yourself when you lose somebody you love (not necessarily to death: a simple breakup will do). That, in the effort to recover what you have lost, you go vainly back to the places you have visited with the beloved, looking as much for your former self as for your missing other half. That your next attempt at love will have in it a much greater measure of will: having been tricked by chance, or luck, or fate, you are less able to relax into its hands the next time around. That, despite this excess of will, your next love affair will follow roughly the same pattern as your last one, because you have *not* really lost yourself—your essential character is all too much with you still, preventing you from being other than you have always been. That lovers are selfish and demanding: they wish to remake the beloved in the image of their own desire, and any deviation from that ideal will irk them. That the person you think you love may not be that person at all. That it is easier to be in love with fictional characters (or dreams, or visions, or images) than it is with real, down-to-earth people. That love is mysterious and archaic, with something almost ghostly about it, so that being powerfully in love seems to take you back to some point of origin, back beyond your childhood to a past you couldn't actually have known. "We are soul mates"; "I seem to have known him forever": these are the banal, colloquial expressions of a feeling that *Vertigo,* with all its dramatic excess, subtly and skillfully captures.

At the heart of the movie is a ghost story that doesn't really exist—not just in the obvious sense that ghosts themselves don't exist, but because it has largely been made up by a character in the movie. Seeking to get rid of his rich wife and safely inherit her wealth, Gavin Elster constructs the tale of Carlotta Valdes, a long-dead woman whose spirit is now haunting Madeleine Elster, driving her toward madness and suicide. Since he can't get his real wife to cooperate in this plot (and in fact we never even see the real Madeleine Elster in this movie—but what does "real" mean, when we are talking about an invisible, offstage, fictional character?), Elster hires a young woman named Judy to impersonate her. And since he needs an audience for the story, he hires Jimmy Stewart—or John "Scotty" Ferguson, as the movie calls him—to follow his pretend wife and observe her strange behavior.

Gavin, a clever fellow, doesn't make the Carlotta story up wholesale: he weaves in bits and pieces of reality, the better to fool his own private detective. So Scotty learns from a local antiquarian that there was indeed a Carlotta Valdes, a San Francisco woman who was abandoned by her rich lover, and whose grave can be found in the cemetery at Mission Dolores. This part of the story is true in the sense that Gavin didn't make it up; it is true, that is, in the context of the movie, which is itself a made-up story about things that happened in San Francisco. As Scotty discovers, there is also a portrait hanging in the Palace of the Legion of Honor called *Portrait of Carlotta,* and the woman he takes to be Madeleine Elster noticeably resembles it, down to the rosebud bouquet she carries, the twist she puts into her chignon, and the strikingly individual piece of jewelry she wears around her neck. (Just think of the work Gavin Elster had to go through to get all the pieces to fit credibly together: the historical research, the plot construction, the costuming and hairstyling, the mingling of the found and useful with the created and necessary props. Hitchcock is admiring, and self-admiring.)

Gavin tells Scotty that Madeleine is Carlotta's great-granddaughter, and that she inherited some of Carlotta's jewelry. But when we realize—late in the movie, though before Scotty himself does—that the whole mad-Madeleine story has been a con job, we also realize that the necklace must be a fake, a piece of costume jewelry commissioned by Gavin to match the necklace in the portrait. (There is nothing in the historical record to suggest that the Carlotta of the museum portrait is actually Carlotta Valdes; part of Gavin's cleverness has been to put those two disparate pieces of reality together.) The necklace may be a worthless fake, but it is also a piece with tremendous sentimental value for Judy, who has kept it to remind herself of those few days as Madeleine, when she and Scotty were in love. It is this necklace that she puts on to let Scotty know—consciously or unconsciously, the movie never tells us—that the Madeleine he lost and the Judy he has now are in fact the same person.

Like Judy, we in the audience continue to hold on to something from the Carlotta plot even though it has been proven a fake. This particular Hitchcock gimmick is the very opposite of a MacGuffin: it is a story element so powerful that even after it has ceased to function in the mystery it persists in ghostly form in our imaginations. It is bigger than Gavin Elster, who created it, and much bigger than Judy, who embodied it. When we think about Kim Novak in this movie, it is Madeleine we remember, not Judy. (Kim Novak was never used so well in any other movie, before or since. If Hitchcock simply drew on what was there in Jimmy Stewart —what he knew was there, from earlier films like *The Man Who Knew Too Much* and *Rope*—he made something entirely new out of Kim Novak.) And because Madeleine exerts this powerful hold on us—from beyond the grave, as it were— we understand not just why Scotty can't love Judy for her down-to-earth self, but also why Madeleine herself can't let go of Carlotta. So the made-up story of a woman inhabited by her own dead ancestress comes to be as real, or as important, as the central love plot doubly enacted by Jimmy Stewart. "As" is not really the right connective here: they lend each other importance because they are in some way the same plot. The longing to be haunted by something richer and more mystical than one's own daily existence—that is what *Vertigo* so cunningly enables us to feel. You can call it romantic love, or the movies, or fiction, or ghosts, or history (*Vertigo*, at various times, calls it all of these), but whatever you decide to call it, you will not be able to rationalize it away by pointing to its invisibility, its patent nonpalpability. Whatever it is, it is there even when it is not there.

At about the time I saw *Vertigo* in that afternoon showing for Ed Snow's class, it became popular to view this film as a movie about moviemaking. For all I know, this is the domi-

nant view still, at least among film buffs. And it would be idiotic to deny that the movie contains those elements; I have
even pointed to some of them, in my comments on Gavin Elster as film director. But to argue that *Vertigo* is exclusively or
even largely about filmmaking is like arguing that Shakespeare's plays are primarily about playwriting or Wordsworth's Immortality Ode about poetical powers. If they
were only about these things, we would long ago have
ceased to care about them (except, perhaps, for the few people actually engaged in these fields—and even filmmakers
and playwrights and poets, one hopes, occasionally think
about other things than their work). You can come up with
lots of ideas about the self-referentially filmic aspects of *Vertigo*, but you can only really *feel* the moments that are about
love, or loss, or being inhabited by something or someone
else—all those things I thought the movie was about when
it affected me so powerfully at the age of twenty-four.

I have seen the movie four or five times since then, and no
viewing has been quite so overwhelming as that second one.
(*Vertigo* is, after all, about second chances, and second
chances only: there is magic in that number two.) But I have
never seen it without noticing or feeling something new. It is
a movie that never goes dead on me—though, granted, I
have made sure not to see it too frequently, not to let it fade
into an annual cliché like *It's a Wonderful Life* or *Peter Pan*.
With the exception of one videotape viewing, when I was
writing about *Vertigo* in the late 1980s for my second book, I
have let the movie come to me on its own schedule, as it did
when I first saw it.

This most recent time, it happened to be on television, in
a beautifully reconstructed print, on a channel with no commercials. My husband noticed it in the daily listings as he
was casting about for something for us to watch on TV, and
read it out almost jokingly—as if assuming we couldn't possibly watch *that* again, because we had just seen it together a

few years earlier, and before that each of us had seen it many times on our own. The last time we'd seen it, the newly restored print was playing at the Castro Theater in San Francisco, which is one of the few perfectly maintained movie palaces from cinema's glamorous era, a place where it is always a pleasure to see an old film, especially an old film about San Francisco. That time, we had taken our son, as part of what we felt was his necessary education. He has since become a cinephile of excessive proportions, as perhaps only adolescents can be, and this time he was out at a movie himself—possibly even his second movie of the day —while we were at home watching *Vertigo* on TV. All this was in my mind as I sat down to watch it. I was aware, that is, of the way in which the movie marked off certain milestones in my life, so that I was one kind of wife and mother the last time I saw it, a different kind (a later, older kind) this time. And of course I had not been a wife or a mother at all the first time I saw it, or the second, or even the third.

I had all along planned to write about *Vertigo* for this book, and now here it was—my designated rereading, in the form of this spontaneous re-seeing. I thought of taking notes, and then thought better of it. With anything as fast-moving as a movie—for that matter, with anything at all that has its own pace, whether it's a dance performance or a lecture or a film—I can't have the full experience and record it at the same time. I wanted to immerse myself once again in *Vertigo*, have the intense version of the experience: that seemed more important than any details about color schemes (though the color schemes are breathtaking) or musical structure (though the music is essential to the mood of each scene) that I might hope to capture in notes. Besides, I had seen the movie so many times that I figured I could remember the crucial scraps of dialogue, if I needed them. So I just watched it. But I watched it in a state of alert readiness, looking in particular for anything new, anything I hadn't noticed before. And I also tried to watch it in a state of passive receptivity, which meant watching myself for my emotional response, observing how the movie had its effect on me this time around — because it is never the same twice.

Over the years, I have come to be more and more interested in the figure of Midge, the Barbara Bel Geddes character who is hopelessly in love with Scotty (or Johnny, as she calls him: they have known each other since college, so she uses his more intimate name). This time, I was more than ever aware of the painfulness of that role. There is the pain that she feels — she humiliates herself, for instance, by mocking Scotty's love for Madeleine/Carlotta with a grotesque, parodic self-portrait — and the pain that she inflicts on us by being, through no fault of her own, the wrong woman. She is kin to that wide-faced, bespectacled girl or woman who runs all the way through Hitchcock's American period (sometimes, horrifyingly, he had his daughter play the role): the wife to be murdered in *Strangers on a Train,* the little sister in *Shadow of a Doubt,* possibly even Cary Grant's disapproving mother in *North by Northwest.* There is a great deal of the mother about Midge's relationship to Scotty ("Mother's here" are among her last words to him, spoken as he sits, zombie-like, in the mental hospital), and also something sisterly in the way she jokes with him about love and sex. She is, in other words, off limits as a sexual partner, and yet she desperately wants to be one. That is a big part of the discomfort she creates in us — that, and her persistent perkiness. We like her, I think, but we also want her to be gone: she is an impediment to the Scotty-Madeleine plot, which consumes all our interest (as it consumes all of Scotty's). Yet there is something sad and almost admirable about Midge in our last vision of her, which I only noticed this time around — the way she walks away from us down a long corridor, the camera holding itself still as she moves out of the light and into a gradually deepening obscurity. It is a bit like the corridor Madeleine (or rather, Judy posing as Madeleine posing as Carlotta) describes walking down in her imagination, the one that will end in madness and suicide.

Scotty, too, has a moment with a corridor, only his is a dream moment, and he is falling downward into a refracted tunnel, an *Alice in Wonderland*–like rabbit hole, but with square corners. Because it is a dream (especially a Hitchcock dream), the image is stylized, and Scotty's body is just a black silhouette of Jimmy Stewart, his hands held open helplessly by his sides, his legs slightly apart. We think, when we see this dream, that it is about his own fear of falling—his vertigo. But the last image of the movie (and this, too, I just noticed for the first time) is of Jimmy Stewart in exactly that pose, standing on the ledge outside the bell tower at San Juan Batista, looking down on Judy's fallen body. So the helplessness of the pose is not fear of his *own* death, but despair at the death he has once again brought about, the third falling death he has been involved in, if you count the policeman as well as Madeleine and Judy. His vertigo, it seems, is finally cured (at least, he stands on that ledge for a good long moment without quailing or fainting), but at too high a cost. The fear it represented all along was not about himself; he, it turns out, was always safe. Only those around him were at risk, while he was destined to survive and repeat the cycle. It is the fear of that repetition—having to go through it all over again, the same and yet not the same—that is embodied in his vertigo. There is a version of this sensation that can be thrilling (the thrill Borges feels when he contemplates *Don Quixote*, the chill that Wordsworth's Ode gives me), but in Hitchcock, as usual, the thrill has been pushed over the edge of pleasurable excitement into the region of fear.

The fear of repetition and the lure of repetition: these are the two poles between which the movie vibrates. Scotty is a man who is doomed to repeat himself—even verbally, it seems. "I look up, I look down. I look up, I look down," he says as he is practicing on Midge's stepladder; or "You're my second chance, Judy, you're my second chance." Randall Jarrell said of the husband in Robert Frost's "Home Burial" that "if one knew only this man one would say, 'Man is the animal that repeats.'" But in *Vertigo* it's not just the one man; the symptom is contagious. Midge, too, begins to repeat: "Stupid! Stupid! Stupid!" she accuses herself, as she destroys the grotesque portrait that has angered Scotty. The verbal tic is not just a tic. It is symptomatic of the way people in this movie live their lives.

But then, no detail in a Hitchcock movie is "just" a tic. The pieces all fit together as a perfect, seamless whole, with each element contributing its bit toward the larger picture. Unlike other thriller directors, Hitchcock does not make mistakes. If you go back over the movie once the disguises and tricks have been ripped away, you won't find any unexplained, inexplicable plot elements, any useless or dishonest red herrings.

Or will you? This time through, for the very first time, I thought I had found one. When Scotty tracks Madeleine to the McKittredge Hotel, he watches her go in and then sees her part a curtain in the upstairs front room. Leaving his parked car and entering the hotel himself, he asks the woman at the front desk about the occupant of that upstairs room. Yes, her name is Carlotta Valdes, such a sweet thing, no, she doesn't sleep there, just comes to the room to sit several times a week. But no, she's not there now, hasn't been seen coming in or out all day. Scotty makes the desk clerk go up and check: the room is empty, and when he looks outside, Madeleine's car is gone.

There are many possible explanations for this scene that do not involve ghosts. The woman at the front desk could have been inattentive or even momentarily absent. But then how did Madeleine get out without passing by Scotty? There could be a back door, but the movie doesn't mention one. Alternatively, Scotty could have imagined seeing her tweak the curtain—he's certainly in a dreamy state by this time—so maybe she never went up to the room at all. But if that's the case, how did he correctly identify her room? Perhaps she climbed out a second-story window while he was inside and scurried down the fire escape. This is possible, but very un–Hitchcock, very un–Kim Novak. More to the point, the movie never offers us *any* of these explanations, or anything else to replace them. Later, when we learn that Gavin Elster set up the whole plot, we are told or can figure out how he did almost everything. But we can never figure out how he managed this ghostly disappearance of Madeleine.

The effect of this, at least on me, is not to damage the powerful perfection of the movie, as a true mistake would do. There are, after all, rational explanations if we want to make them up ourselves. Instead, this little moment is one of the things that enable the Madeleine part of the story to live beyond its strict confines. Ghostly evasions of reality, perpetuations of characters who never existed, events without explanations, all feed the hungry imagination, making it feel that there is more to life than just the stuff we can see and understand. And this, in turn, makes the repetitions inherent in life (and books, and the movies) more bearable. Yes, we are all trapped in a cycle, and yes, we will just get the same pattern repeated over and over again. But the trap isn't absolutely closed, the pattern isn't seamless—there are cracks and rips that might, if we are lucky, result in somebody escaping after all. Madeleine-Carlotta is only Gavin Elster's creation, but she might succeed in getting away from him anyway. If we credit the ghostly (even if we only credit it with the part of our minds reserved for fiction), then the possibilities for escape become much more plentiful.

My own ghost, in relation to this movie—my own Carlotta, if you will—is San Francisco. Watching *Vertigo* this time, I felt more strongly than anything else a pang for that lost city of my youth. Those shots of the city as a whole, in which Coit Tower was the tallest structure on the horizon: that was the San Francisco of my childhood. And even in the days when I first knew the man who is now my husband, and we claimed the entire city as our pleasure-haunt and place of refuge, San Francisco was more like its old self than its new one—more like the vision in Hitchcock's movie than the traffic-filled, skyscraper-shaded place it is now.

Like Scotty, I am mourning a beloved who never really existed. San Francisco was certainly very beautiful (it still is, compared with most places), but it was never exactly like the city in *Vertigo*. I don't just mean that Hitchcock has played fast and loose with the street patterns and the views out windows, though he has notoriously done that. I don't even mean that he has made the colors richer and the streets cleaner and the parking easier than they ever were in real life; all movies do that sort of thing. I guess I mean that the San Francisco whose loss I now feel so intensely is not the one I actually walked and drove around in, but the one I came to know and remember through my successive viewings of *Vertigo*.

Take Ernie's, for instance, the restaurant where Scotty first saw Madeleine, and where he took Judy on their first date. Ernie's was there all throughout my youth and far into my adulthood. The decor remained exactly as it had been in the 1950s; the food was reportedly terrible. I could have eaten there any number of times (my husband and I even considered it, on one of our jaunts around the city), but I never did. The only reason it had any meaning for me was its appearance in *Vertigo*. And yet now that the restaurant has closed—now that it doesn't actually exist on Montgomery Street, across from the old Melvin Belli law office, which also doesn't exist anymore—I clutch my heart when I see it in the movie and think, "Oh, Ernie's!"

The same, or something similar, is true of the Palace of the Legion of Honor. It's a lovely spot with some nice paintings in its collection, but do I ever go there? When I do go, what I always do first, almost instinctively, is to peek into that long room to the left of the central foyer, hoping to see what I know will not be there: the *Portrait of Carlotta* that Hitchcock commissioned just for the movie. Come to think of it, I've probably been to that museum more in the movie than I have in real life—that is, my visits to the Palace over the last forty years do not exceed the number of times I've seen *Vertigo*. And yet it too, as a physical place in San Francisco, feels important to me now. I'm also unreasonably attached to the flower-seller Podesta Baldocchi, which originally occupied a downtown alley off Grant (roughly where Hitchcock had it), then moved out to the Avenues, and finally left the city for the suburbs. In real life, does this matter to me one whit? Did I even once buy flowers there? No, and no. But I always liked seeing the store and remembering how Madeleine had gone into it to buy her bouquet. So I miss it tremendously, now that I am watching the movie once again.

The places of our childhood are like the books of our youth: that's essentially what Henry James and Mark Twain are saying, each in his own way, in the passages I quoted at the beginning of this book. But both those authors are talking about an actual home—"the parental threshold and hearth-stone," "the house of his childhood"—whereas I am talking about something slightly different.

I have, since starting this book, been back to the Palo Alto house of *my* childhood, just to look at it from the outside. It is inhabited by strangers now (though the original next-door neighbors are still there, and one of them even came out of her garage door and recognized me on the street, surprising both of us). I stood there, waiting for the Mark Twain effect, the Henry James effect, but to no avail. Perhaps I was resisting; perhaps that house on Ben Lomond Drive contained too many memories I didn't want to recall. But for whatever reasons, my emotions failed to render up the appropriate response. Standing in front of my old house, I did not feel it had shrunk, nor did I find it filled with old associations, "figured, gilded, and enriched." Unlike the books of my youth, it did not reflect back to me any self I recognized. I couldn't, in short, reread it.

But San Francisco is another matter. Because it entered my imagination the way *I Capture the Castle* or *Paradise Lost* did—as a place that was already half-dreamed, presented to me as an artist's vision—it can mirror for me the different stages of my life and my character. Aided by Hitchcock, I can see in the city both alteration and permanence. The vertigo, for me, lies precisely in that gap between the unchanging object (the city in the movie, the movie itself) and the ever changing reality I inhabit, including my own body and my own personality.

Once I was a ten-year-old child whose life was almost all imagined future. Now I am a middle-aged adult with a substantial past to remember. I am utterly altered and yet still somehow the same, and I know this because there in my memory are the books I once read (and the movies I watched, and the paintings I saw), waiting to be taken out and looked at anew. The view from here is a different one, but there is also something familiar about it. That, I suppose, is what makes the process of rereading at once so pleasurable and so unnerving. I have loved being surrounded by my ghosts in this way. I will be sorry to let them go.

INDEX